OUTBACK RAMBLING

OUTBACK RAMBLING

RICHARD SYMANSKI

THE UNIVERSITY OF ARIZONA PRESS   TUCSON

The University of Arizona Press

Copyright © 1990
Richard Symanski
All Rights Reserved

This book was set in 9½/12½ CRT Trump Mediaeval.
⊗ This book is printed on acid-free, archival-quality paper.
Manufactured in the United States of America.
95 94 93 92 91 90   5 4 3 2 1

LIBRARY OF CONGRESS CATALOGING-IN-PUBLICATION DATA

Symanski, Richard.
    Outback rambling / Richard Symanski.
        p.   cm.
    Includes bibliographical references (p   ).
    ISBN 0-8165-1167-5 (alk. paper)
        1. Northern Territory—Description and travel.   2. Symanski,
Richard—Journeys—Australia—Northern Territory.
DU395.S96   1990
914.2904'63—dc20   89-20675
                                                          CIP

British Library Cataloguing in Publication data are available.

Two essays in this book were originally published in *Focus*,
a magazine of the American Geographical Society, and are
reprinted by permission: "A Sidelong Look at Alice" (Vol. 37,
No. 2) and "When Rabbits Run Wild" (Vol. 38, No. 2).

FOR TYE

CONTENTS

PREFACE

In the antipodean fall of 1965 I hitchhiked from Melbourne to Port Augusta, where I got a ticket in last class on the Ghan train for the eight-hundred-mile trip by rail to Alice Springs. I can still recall waking in the middle of the night aboard the click-clacking Ghan with my head on an Aboriginal woman's lap, my legs tangled in dusty sacks of emu meat, my whiteness and touch-presence the objects of charming, cavernous-eyed black children. I remember being mesmerized by patches of silvery mulga and tulip-shaped witchetty bush, hopping mobs of six-foot red kangaroos, baked orange earth strewn with sharp pebbles that spread like a gigantic tablecloth to the limits of my vision.

I recall an oppressively hot afternoon in The Alice when I was chided by hard-drinking yahoos and station cowboys for having had a beer in the wrong part of the pub, among lowly barefoot "coons." Nor will I ever forget the flies that seemed as common as stars on a commonplace Alice night. They perched on eyelids, they tickled parched lips, they made white T-shirts look like roofing material. And how could anyone forget the sight of scores of bedraggled Aborigines sleeping and seeking shelter beneath humpies and lean-tos in the sandy bottom of the Todd River?

I knew little about Australia then, even less about the history behind the pathetic degradation of Aborigines. I knew nothing about all the splendid wildlife—the emus, the 'roos, the parrots—that I was seeing for the very first time.

In the winter of 1986 I again found myself in Australia, but now I was a different person. I'd taught in several North American universities, cavorted with professional biologists and social scientists, traveled extensively in North America and Latin America, and found myself doing research and writing on everything from Colombian peasants, Dominican Jews and illegal aliens to zonked-out big-city whores and wild horses.

Before arriving in Alice Springs I'd heard that there were a couple of hundred thousand wild horses roaming free in arid Australia. I'd convinced myself that I didn't want to do more research on horses. I'd spent a couple of years looking at the social and political environment of mustang management in the American West, and after the publication of my book, *Wild Horses and Sacred Cows*, in 1985, I thought it was time to move on to something new.

Once in the Outback, however, I was sought out for my expertise on feral horses. I was hired by the Conservation Commission of the Northern Territory to research and write a piece for a national newspaper on damage being done by the horses and on how the problem should be solved. During and after this venture I came into contact with just about all of the Centre's major scientists and conservationists. I was able to pick their brains, see problems and priorities through their eyes, gain their confidence, get introductions to cattlemen and leads to sources of information that I could not have found on my own.

On my own—at least initially—I tried to learn what I could about the Centre's Aborigines. Here barriers are clearly formidable; language and a wide cultural chasm preclude all but a few outsiders from really getting to know Aborigines. Except for anthropologists who spend extended periods of time with Aborigines, what one learns about them comes through visual impressions, reflections on one's own culture, local gossip and half-truths, history books and mimeographed manuscripts. Still, since some Aboriginal issues cannot be separated from conservation issues and from the reality of white hegemony over land

and resources, I could not help but form opinions about a narrow band of native concerns.

If there is a common theme in this book it is, I think, a pivotal concern with land (as an irreplaceable resource), with life (wildlife, native life and introduced life), and with the sorts of accommodations and maladaptations that have resulted when Europeans have imposed themselves upon an alien environment and upon a technologically inferior people easily subjugated. A couple of the chapters are unabashedly descriptive; I was after no more than a mood, a feeling, the experience.

Abbreviated versions of "The Horses Must Be Killed" and "Returning to the Land" first appeared in *The Australian, Hoofs and Horns* (Australia), and *The Bulletin* (Australia).

This book could not have been written without the kind assistance of many people, chief among them Dave Berman, Mandy Bowman, John Brumbie, Bob Crogan, Gary Dan, Bob Fox, Ron Hooper, Ken Johnson, Dick Kimber, Bill Low, Steve Morton, Des Nelson, Graham Pearce, Stuart Philpott, Bob Purvis, D. L. Smith, Mark Stafford Smith, Sonia Tidemann, Chris Torlach, and Jim Turner. I also am indebted to numerous Aborigines and cattle station owners and managers who took time to answer questions and to acquaint me with their world. Nancy Burley alone knows the special debt I owe her.

OUTBACK RAMBLING

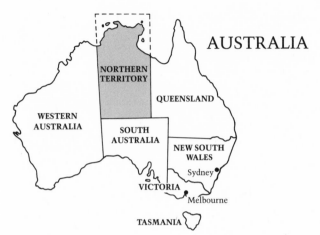

AUSTRALIA

WESTERN
AUSTRALIA

NORTHERN
TERRITORY

QUEENSLAND

SOUTH
AUSTRALIA

NEW SOUTH
WALES

Sydney

VICTORIA

Melbourne

TASMANIA

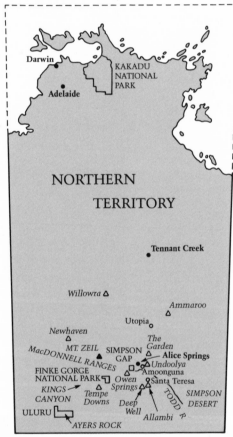

Darwin

KAKADU
NATIONAL
PARK

Adelaide

NORTHERN

TERRITORY

- TOWNS AND CITIES

△ CATTLE STATIONS

□ PARKS

o ABORIGINAL SETTLEMENTS
AND FREEHOLDS

Tennant Creek

Willowra △

Ammaroo
△

Utopia o

Newhaven
△

The
Garden

MT. ZEIL   SIMPSON
GAP

Alice Springs

MacDONNELL RANGES

Undoolya
△

FINKE GORGE
NATIONAL PARK □

Owen
Springs △

Amoonguna
△ Santa Teresa

KINGS →
CANYON

Tempe
Downs

Deep
Well

TODD R

SIMPSON
DESERT

ULURU □

Allambi

AYERS ROCK

IMAGINING
THE OUTBACK

Imagine a land where you can drive for hours and not see a gas station, a bar, a billboard, another car, a single person. Now imagine a mob of fifteen or twenty emus galloping toward the horizon; a lone dingo silently prowling the sandy edges of a dry riverbed edged with river red gums; a red kangaroo standing on its hind legs beside an acacia tree, as motionless as a meditating monk; a pair of Major Mitchell cockatoos preening one another atop a nine-story gum tree, and, on the other side of the road, a thousand brilliantly green budgerigars clouding the sky like a locust plague. For the whole of this pitted red track of a road that goes on and on you can't begin to imagine how many other kinds of birds you've seen, how many tens of thousands of brown and tan spire-like termite mounds you've passed, how many hundreds of millions of ants plow this land.

This is the Australian Outback.

But there are other outbacks, many of them. Drive onto a station road and head for the homestead. Along the way you'll come upon spent inner tubes, green and blue beer cans, old cars turned upside down and riddled with bullets, a field canvassed with stunning yellow flowers that shock the senses like a flashlight beamed into the eyes on a moonless night, a stately wedge-tailed eagle with a nine-foot wingspan keenly devouring a cow that died of thirst or hunger. Creep past the opportunistic carnivore, then pick up speed and roll on into a red dust storm that leaps from the sandy track. Coughing, slowing, edging to the left side of the track, gaze at the belching Chevrolet with a shattered windshield that zooms by you, a glaring pink sedan loaded with a dozen shouting, smiling, laughing, waving Aborigines.

Now, off on your left, you see a heavenly ghost gum as white as chalk; it's marred by graffiti, filled with screeching galahs, home to a rusted oil can nailed to an arching limb. Farther on, on your left, a hundred yards to the south, lies a stockyard. On one side is a motionless windmill, on the other several thorny corkwoods and drooping ironwoods sing with winged life. For hundreds of yards around the stockyard everything that resembles plant life looks gnawed, trampled, beaten into submission. You look harder, searching for life. In a massive tangle of half-dead prickly wattle you see several shorthorns with their mouths to the ground.

Drive for hours through the Outback, through a rainbow of earthbound colors that vary all the way from lilac and henna to copper and scarlet, and you begin to sense that something's amiss, something doesn't fit with your North American upbringing. You've seen no more than a small stand or two of oaks or pines; you've seen none of the deciduous trees so commonplace in your continent's center. Now pause for a long minute and observe the trees and bushes, the leathery, spiny, hard leaves. Everywhere you look, you soon realize, there's almost nothing but acacias and eucalypts—gums to Aussies. Almost all of them, several hundred species of each, are native to this part of the world. Eighty percent of Australia's plants are endemic to the continent.

Drop your eyes to the ground and something else strikes you as peculiar. Much of the land you've been traveling through is covered with a round, hummocky plant that looks hostile and half dead, and is as prickly as it appears from afar. This is spinifex. It covers a third of the Outback and is the most extensive vegetation type in Australia. Virtually inedible to all large herbivores, with the exception of the euro, or hill kangaroo, and to dozens of smaller ones, spinifex grasslands harbor immense numbers of termites and the richest array of lizard species anywhere in the world.

Follow an Aboriginal woman with crowbar in hand into a clump of mulga trees. Admire her patience as she gets down on her knees and digs down a foot or two into the red earth in search of honey ants to satisfy her craving for sugar. When she comes upon one with a distended abdomen the size of a grape, she holds it by the head and puts the abdomen between her lips and sucks the sweetness into her mouth. Were she to dig all day long she might find as many as two thousand ants in thirty or more chambers.

Wander into The Other Place in Alice Springs anytime after four in the afternoon. On your way to the bar and a beer, squirm through a crowd of noisy and sweaty regulars clad in rumpled tank tops, cut-off blue jeans, slacks heavy with dust, cheap dresses. The regulars are twenty, forty, fifty; they're white, they're brown from too much sun, they're shades of black and brown from racial mixing. Male or female, whatever the age, these habitués love earrings, tattoos, four-letter words, ribald stories, fights, drinking—most of all drinking. They live in town, on cattle stations, in Aboriginal town camps. They work in construction, mend fences, drill for oil, recycle garbage, drive huge road trains. They live on the dole.

Walk out of The Other Place and around the corner onto Todd Street, into camera shops, bookstores, supermarkets, Aboriginal agencies, tourist shops, a Kentucky Fried Chicken franchise, an Aboriginal art gallery. People all along the tree-studded mall are neat and clean, genteel, middle class, young, adventuresome, in the late autumn of their lives. They're locals. They're from everywhere: Munich, Long Beach, Milan, Atlanta, Sydney, Tokyo, Cape Town, near and far Aboriginal outstations.

After a while in the Outback, images multiply. There are hundreds, thousands, more. There are as many different possible descriptions and characterizations of Outback Australia as there are people with open eyes and curious minds. Some images and impressions come easily, others emerge slowly, after you've wandered and meddled, become privy to what might be called facts, after you've gotten a hold on loose but feel-right generalities. I have a handful of special images of the Outback. More than others that come to mind when I think of Australia's vast interior, they define the place, make it concrete, different, unforgettable, an indelible region in my mind.

How could I not be struck by a couple of straightforward geographical facts about the Centre? Distances from one point of human activity to another are considerable by any standard. A 100- or 200-mile trip is short, one of 500 miles nothing to complain about. Such distances are understandable. The Northern Territory is twice the size of Texas, ten times that of Illinois, seventy times larger than Massachusetts. But the Territory has a mere 140,000 people, which is less than one-tenth the population of Houston, no more than a couple of decent-sized Chicago suburbs.

Equally striking is how the population is distributed. Almost half the Territory's people live in a single city, Darwin. Situated in the humid tropics, its collective mind set on Asia, Darwin possesses an ethnic diversity perhaps unparalleled anywhere in a city of its size. Alice Springs, more than a thousand miles distant, accounts for another 25,000 or so people. The Aboriginal nerve center of the continent, isolated from all places and yet a destination for almost all tourists, Alice has almost nothing in common with Darwin. Subtract Darwin and Alice Springs from the Territory's population and you have the equivalent of the students of a Big Ten college claiming an area the size of California, Washington, Oregon, Idaho, and Utah combined.

Cattle stations, or ranches in the American idiom, are, like the Outback itself, equally vast and equally empty. Holdings of 1,000 to 1,400 square miles are commonplace. Such stations, with 4,000 to 6,000 head of cattle, support no more than a family of four or five and perhaps a couple of helpers. So huge are these stations that until quite recently, when cattle had to be tested for brucellosis and tuberculosis and fences were required, owners could only guess at how many cattle they had. Rarely did they know the real number. There are instances in the Territory in which the buyer of a cattle station found so many additional livestock on his land that the unexpected windfall was enough to pay off the mortgage. One authentic story has it that when a cattleman bought a large station in the northern reaches of the Territory he told the seller that he'd buy him a beer for every cow he found that exceeded the number claimed in the sales agreement. At last count he owed the seller 11,000 cans, and he still hadn't finished mustering all of the station's livestock.

A little known fact about the Centre is that it's home to well over a million feral animals, descendants of domesticated creatures brought to Australia in the nineteenth century. Indeed, there are so many unwanted introduced animals here that there's simply no other place on Earth like it. There are hundreds of thousands of feral pigs in the Territory's Top End. A quarter of a million water buffalo, more than half of all those free-roaming in the world today, are spread over 60,000 square miles of coastal floodplains and woodlands in The Top End. Pigs and buffalo alike do immense damage. In the richest waterbird habitats in Australia they trample and destroy native species, they accelerate soil erosion, they increase saltwater intrusion into freshwater habitats, they scar the land with wallows and trails. And buffalo carry diseases like tuberculosis. There's an industry in buffalo hides and meat for human consumption, and in the early 1990s the large animals—bulls can weigh up to 2,500 pounds—will be fenced in and controlled just as cattle are today. There's no market for the pigs. They're shot all the time, by anyone with a gun and nothing better to do. They're impossible to get rid of.

No one has any idea of how many feral cats prosper in the Territory. There could be tens of thousands of them, more. Nor does anyone know how massive a toll they've taken on small native mammals and bird life. It's alleged that many of the cats weigh upwards of ten or twelve pounds.

Yet another European pest that numbers in the hundreds of thousands in the Outback is the rabbit. Its numbers fluctuate wildly, depending on rainfall and feed in certain habitats. Unlike feral cats, rabbits don't kill small natives directly, but they do a thoroughgoing job of destroying plants on which native wildlife depend for sustenance. Some scientists intimate with the Outback argue that no single animal has been more destructive than the lowly little rabbit in changing pre-European environments. In the southern reaches of the Territory, on the sandhill portions of cattle stations and especially in the forbidding Simpson Desert, perhaps as many as 40,000 feral dromedary camels range at will. They're the grandchildren and greatgrandchildren of the camels that proved so indispensable in the early exploration and settlement of the dry interior. Once roads were put in and trucks became available, they could be forgotten. Many were set free, and like all the other large and small alien animals in the Outback that broke loose or were released from their domestic environments, camels took to the wild to multiply wantonly.

Then there are the feral horses. Little more than a decade ago they were thought to number about 50,000, a population comparable to that found in the American West today. Now it's known that the true figure may be closer to 250,000. In a generous definition of the Centre, to include the immense arid portions of Western Australia, Queensland, New South Wales, South Australia, and most of the Northern Territory, the figure may be 500,000. Feral horses are taking an enormous toll on remote environments, on soils, on remaining native plants and small animals.

To outsiders and residents of the Outback alike, the kinds of numbers I have put forth seem preposterous, the drunken inventions of a madman with a hidden agenda. From bitumen roads and dirt tracks throughout the Outback one rarely sees more than an occasional band of horses or donkeys, an elusive cat, or, with great luck, a small herd of camels. Nowhere does one come upon these animals in numbers that would suggest populations of the sort now known to exist. Even from a helicopter the landscape seems surprisingly bereft of most of these destructive intruders. This, however, is not as strange as it seems; rather it is just one more testament to a simple and inescapable fact of geography: size. Spread a million feral animals evenly over the Territory and you'll only find one about every one-half square mile. Put these same feral animals anywhere beyond a couple of hundred yards of the few roads that cut through the Outback and you'll be lucky to see any one of them every 25 to 50 miles.

Locate them in habitats they most prefer and you'll have a difficult time seeing them even from a low-flying helicopter.

The phenomenal impact of all of these foreigners on the Outback's native flora and fauna cannot be underestimated. Yet it is European man—Englishmen primarily—who have done the most to permanently alter the face of the Centre. A blatant frontier mentality reigns virtually everywhere in the Outback. Pastoralists and miners, businessmen and government bureaucrats are there to reap as much as they can as quickly as they can. With the notable exception of Aborigines, few have a strong attachment to place, much less to the land. In fact, statistics bear out that most white people in the Centre are tied to this or that place with about as much permanence as the ephemeral waters that quickly come and go in the perennially dry rivers of the Outback. Not surprisingly, there is very little understanding of or regard for anyone's future generations. And if somewhere in the Outback—even among those who can trace their lineage back more than a hundred years—there is a land ethic worthy of the name, its whereabouts is as elusive as the Holy Grail.

Despite the relentless environmental rape of a good portion of a continent the size of the U.S. excluding Alaska, there is still enough exotic and captivating bird life in the Outback to make a sojourner from North America green with envy. In the early mornings, in the afternoons, at dusk, around anything that provides open water, the delights mesmerize. They could enthrall an imaginative mind forever. Mating, singing, fighting, flocking, screeching, swooping—one needs a thesaurus to capture all the exhilarating behaviors, the combinations of colors, all of this life on the wing so close to one's eyes. One doesn't need to be a birder or a biologist to know that these are special experiences.

If first impressions of the Centre spotlight immensity and emptiness, then later ones arouse thoughts of smallness, claustrophobia, desire for flight. I speak, of course, of sociology, of one's sense of freedom and personal limits, of the feeling that you've come to know too many power brokers and social wags too soon, that you know too much about too many people, that too quickly others have come to know or care too much about you in mischievous ways. Here you lack the freedom that size in numbers—and numbers almost exclusively—guarantees. The Outback is a small-town society.

Australia itself is small, of course, home to a mere 16 million people, Southern California and a little more. But because Australia is urban, the most urban nation in the world, most Aussies need not think small. In the Outback, however, the choice to act big and principled is harder to come by, requires more effort, involves more personal risk. In a small and petty society everyone quickly learns the conservative norm embodied in the old saw: If you want to get along, go along.

The ruling norm in the Outback was laid down by pastoralists, who, after the explorers, were the first whites in this sprawling land. They were the first to subdue the native, to stake out claims that reached beyond the horizons, to proclaim themselves kings forever and all newcomers subject to their rules. To this day no one has effectively overridden the authority of this tiny majority; thus most outback denizens are beholden less to a tested truth of social might than to a long-held belief of where it must reside. It is the rare individual in the Outback, stereotypes notwithstanding, who has the courage to try to change what lies beneath the rotten underbelly of outback Australia: its reactionary politics, its racism, its constant temporizing, its brazen exploitation of all lifeforms.

Just about everything that one sees or feels or senses about the Outback is forcibly skewed by the presence of Aborigines. They evoke guilt for the treatment of all oppressed natives by domineering whites. They force one to think how myopic all of us are in our view of other ways of life. They urge us to consider how land and life in the Outback were exploited in a gentler age; I say gentler not because Aborigines wouldn't have been predisposed to savage the land, although much differently than whites have done, but because for millennia they lived without knowledge of crushingly destructive technologies, because they neither knew of nor had the ability to bring large four-footed herbivores to a land that cannot tolerate them in large numbers.

In the Northern Territory there are some 30,000 Aborigines, and most of them—virtually all full-blood Aborigines—live in a

world quite apart from whites. The races do not mix socially
and they live in geographically separate communities. They
have utterly different conceptions of the physical world, of its
history, of its place in their lives. Aborigines do not see themselves apart from the land. It embodies their distant past, their
ancestors, their most fundamental beliefs, themselves. To
whites the Outback is merely a place to make a living, to
exploit, to destroy as quickly as whim and imagination allow. It
is an adventure, a bus station where you purchase a return ticket
home or to some place else when you arrive.

There is a colossal rift between the Centre's native black inhabitants, who came to Australia tens of thousands of years ago,
and those of Anglo-Celtic origins who presumptuously claimed
all the land as their own little more than a hundred years ago.
The rift is fundamentally racial. It is a rift fed by ignorance and
fear, an assault on the senses that derives from utterly different
values, a barely comprehensible history.

Outback Australia is not South Africa, although even to a
casual observer there are plenty of examples to suggest that a
comparison based on racial injustice is not entirely inappropri-
ate. In towns large and small throughout the Centre, Aborigines
are relentlessly and consistently objects of blatant discrimination: in liquor laws, in access to public facilities, in rights to
land and home ownership, in shameless housing segregation.
Only in the last quarter-century have Australia's Aborigines
been afforded the human rights that whites take for granted.
And it is for little more than a decade that they have been able to
claim land rightfully theirs. Now Aborigines own about thirty
percent of the Northern Territory. This seems most impressive
when it is realized that all their ownership came about since
1976. But one needs to be reminded that from a modern capitalist point of view, almost all Aboriginal lands are marginal,
largely unproductive even for livestock.

Most Aborigines are as uneducated in the ways of a modern
industrial society as they ever were. Now, in a sense, their pre-
dicament is worse than ever. Many suffer from acute alcoholism, from a myriad of stress-induced illnesses, from the erosion
of traditional values. Their population is growing at a phenome-

nally high rate. Giving them land and allowing them to do what they desire without also giving them—especially their children—education and training for life in a society certain to be dominated by whites for as long as one can imagine is a program destined to fail. It is an agenda that will only create an outback version of Harlem without brick and mortar.

The future of the Centre lies in catering to tourists. It lies in satisfying the desires of urban Australians for a vicarious trip into a myth-laden and somewhat imaginary past, the equivalent of North America's equally mythological cowboy West. It lies in satisfying foreigners who have a hankering to see whether the Outback is as remote and strange and beguiling and full of wonderful animal life as hip advertisers and Hollywood would have them believe.

I'm not crazy about any place that defines itself in terms of the ephemeral needs of tourists. And yet tourism may prove to be a great blessing in disguise for the Outback. Even the proliferation of paved highways and billboards and guided tours and the inevitable kitsch and phoniness that already characterize Alice Springs and tiny roadside settlements could prove to be minor costs alongside an eclectic list of benefits. Tourism could open the eyes and minds of people who have the voting power to elect territory and state and federal officials who will enact legislation that brings a new kind of civilized thinking to the Outback—laws that will rid two-thirds of the continent of archaic frontier power bases whose only interest has been brazen short-term exploitation of irreplaceable land and native life; laws that will eliminate many pastoralists and harness the senseless destruction wrought by others; laws that will insure that native flora and fauna have absolute rights and precedence over introduced feral animals; imaginative legislation and humane social programs that will insure that future generations of Aborigines will have the same social and economic rights and opportunities enjoyed by other Australians.

ABORIGINAL
ENCOUNTERS

I climb up to the saddle, pass over the humpy ridge and out of
the glaring light into the shadows of the south side of the mountain. I take out binoculars and find a comfortable spot on a rock
away from the prickly spinifex.

On the western edge of the town camp eight hefty women sit
in a tight circle behind a windbreak, a long sheet of corrugated
iron. They hunch inward, toward the fire, facing one another.
On the other side of the settlement, in a clearing unprotected
from the bracing wind that storms out of the south and funnels
irreplaceable top soil through Heavitree Gap, several men are
gathered in a circle virtually identical in size to that formed by
the women. An old man with a white beard, wearing a wool
coat and a wool cap and no shoes, leans over a shoulder. His lips
move ever so slightly; he motions weakly with his left hand
toward the Stuart Highway. Then, slowly, as if time is of no
consequence, he shambles partway around the circle and begins
speaking to another Aboriginal male.

Is he, I wonder, making arrangements for a modern-day version of an initiation rite invented thousands of years before the
great pyramid of Khufu was imagined? Or is he merely embel-
lishing a mundane story of what happened this day while buying groceries on Todd Street in The Alice?

Hidden behind these magical glasses, my eyes begin wander-
ing through this Aboriginal settlement on the far southern edge
of Alice Springs. I count the Toyota trucks, every one with a

door wide open. I count the cars on blocks and without wheels in front yards. I try to imagine how many fifty-gallon drums would be needed to haul away the garbage strewn everywhere: bean cans, beer cans, bottles, old clothing, rags, shoes. . . .

I sense that it's the garbage more than the small concrete block houses or the yapping multitude of mongrel dogs or the evoked strangeness of these black people that brings me face-to-face with my culture, their culture. I know that anthropologists have described Australian Aborigines as the original throwaway culture. I know that the garbage accumulates from eating non-native foods, the foods least preferred in the Aboriginal hierarchy of things. I know that the absolute quantity of garbage left lying by these people is miniscule alongside that generated by Americans. I know that the backwoods of Vermont and North Carolina and Oregon are full of white people who grew up in the same culture that I did and who let garbage accumulate on their properties just as these Aborigines do. I am no different from other white North Americans and Europeans and Australians who come here; it's the sight of all this garbage in Aboriginal living spaces that catches my eye, holds my attention, encourages me to make value judgments that make me feel uncomfortable.

I backtrack up the ragged slope to the brightly lit side of the saddle. I find a red and grey sandstone rock on which to sit, beneath a wall of burnt orange and deep reds. I face the city's garbage dump, its sanitation pools, the spinifex-splotched MacDonnell Ranges. I slap my neck, then my forehead; I'm bitten several times by mosquitoes. I slap my forearm and a euro off to my right bounds up a crevice and through a pillar of foliating rocks. It's gone before I can adequately judge size, color, sex.

Now a magpie swoops off a high ledge to my right. Its wings strapped tight to its long chest, it speeds earthward, showcasing its elegance. Then, just this side of a ghost gum, it cuts a graceful arc and opens its wings before tracking west.

In the middle distance lies a swamp. It's splotched and ribbed and inked with grasses resplendently spring green, fruit red. In the many-shaped pools, there are hundreds of ducks. Wood ducks? Teals? I'm in the middle of a continent with more than

750 species of birds, as many as in all of North America. A third of them are here in the Centre.

Until recently it was thought that Australia's birds came from Southeast Asia. But scientists who have found biochemical ways to pinpoint how closely species are related to one another have determined that Australia's avifauna have more genetic material in common with one another than they do with their counterparts elsewhere. They are native Australians.

Steve Atkins from Western Australia is ready to go bareback on Heavy Days at the Annual Alice Springs Rodeo when I duck under a rope and head for a stand to buy a beer and a "snag," a sausage sandwich. I inch past a couple of drunk white men in cowboy hats and faded jeans, then round a clump of Aboriginal women sitting on the ground, a castle of beer cans the hub of their social wheel. I shout out my order; it's drowned by a deep voice coming through the loudspeaker announcing that steer-wrestling is the next event. Then Kenny Rogers comes on: "You're the Love of My Life."

I bite into the sausage and grease runs into my beard. I wipe my beard on my shirt sleeve, look up and beyond the sign that reads Don't Remove Liquor from Enclosed Area, and see two Aboriginal youths sneaking under the fence. Dusty shirts and pants in exchange for a free ticket to the rodeo.

I think I should have ordered the other snag, a steak sandwich. Then it occurs to me that this drinking enclosure is a little different from the one on the other side of the stadium. Here a preponderance of Aborigines: men wearing shoes, standing beside their mongrel dogs; women without shoes, without dogs. Off to one side there's a couple of large wire bins for empty beer cans. No one, white or black, seems particularly interested in using them. Drink, Drop and Return to the Action someone seems to have written in invisible ink on the cans.

On the other side of the stadium, near the main entrance, there are few Aborigines, lots of whites: older, gentle, tourists, urbane types. There are no big wire bins, no bastard dogs, no big signs taped to Carlton Draught or Foster's Lager cans about drinking and dropping. Just beyond the cyclone fence in the parking lot there is a Northern Territory paddy wagon, a four-wheel-drive Toyota Land Cruiser with a cage on its chopped bed. I'd seen an Aboriginal man sprawled on the floor inside the cage when I got my first beer. I'll see another when I get my last one late in the day.

"Put your hands together for Sharon McGuire," the announcer shouts, as I move around for a better view from a small rise among a motley lot of Aboriginal men, some with glaring white teeth, others toothless, in Adidas sneakers or cowboy boots, clean-shaven or bearded, round and thick-faced, Caucasian, simian, enthralled, absorbed, laughing. My eyes jump back and forth among these bedraggled men, a calf-roping event, and a hundred or so galahs taking great pleasure in screeching atop ironwoods, now and then zooming back and forth across the show ground.

Without warning I'm jolted from behind, lose my balance, and roll down the rise into a line of five Aborigines, three women and two children. My leg smacks a shoulder, whacks a child's face. I turn and see the force that set me in motion, a well-dressed Aboriginal man in his fifties.

Before I can get to my feet two of the women are cussing and screaming, wildly throwing punches at the man beside me on the ground. In between solid punches and kicks to the face and the groin, the two hefty women's swearing shifts back and forth between some Aboriginal language and English. "Dumb drunken bugger, you!" I hear as I grab for the man's glasses just as they are about to be crushed by a wayward foot. "Go back with your own drunken kind. Get out of here, you bloody no-good bastard!"

Now he takes a slashing kick to the head. I grab him by the arm and yank him toward me. I jump to my feet and help him stand. He has a nasty gash above his right eye; there's blood running down his face. I hand him a handkerchief, then his glasses. He can barely stand. He's drunk.

The Aboriginal women and children look around me, over me, through me. There's no eye contact. I decide that I'm invisible.

Yesterday I was in the town library reading a planning report for Alice Springs. I learned that several places in the town are registered Aboriginal sacred sites. Sacred sites are identifiable landmarks riddled with millennia-old clan and totemic significance. They mark the places where mythic beings first sprang from the earth, or to which they returned at the ends of their journeys. Sacred sites are more than simple reminders of ancestors, for the essence of mythic beings remains in the land, just as it does in animals and plants, in sacred objects, in the bodies of men and women.

Among Alice's numerous Aboriginal sacred sites are Heavitree Gap, Billy Goat Hill, and Anzac Hill. The first is a tracking Dreamtime sacred to men, off-limits to women, and the second a place of female rituals from which men are forbidden. Anzac Hill is a myth-laden place made special by caterpillar men and women who spread over The Alice and its environs and bestowed the land with water and abundant animal life.

Anzac Hill is a prominent crystalline outcrop braided with heavily used trails, disfigured near its modest summit by a spacious parking lot, and topped by a white obelisk, a memorial to the members of the Australian and New Zealand Army Corps who fought and died in the World Wars. From Anzac Hill one gets a good view of Alice's central business district, its commonplace suburbs, its warehouses, Heavitree Gap, and the MacDonnell Ranges. Daily the hill is packed with camera-toting tourists from the farthest reaches of Australia and the world.

I hike to the top of Anzac Hill in search of a plaque commemorating the hill as a sacred site. I find nothing. A mistake, an oversight, I think. It's all covered by uniformed guides in one of the tours that I've not taken.

I walk downtown and visit three tour agencies, all of which advertise a trip to the top of Anzac Hill as a major highlight of The Alice. Agents assure me that I'm mistaken about Anzac Hill being an Aboriginal sacred site. I mention the town planning report. They shrug their shoulders; they say, "Don't know nothing about it."

Maybe a visit to the Northern Territory Tourist Bureau in Todd Street will clarify all this.

"No," I'm told by a sprightly young woman at the tourist bureau. "Anzac Hill is not a sacred site and I bloody well hope it never will be!"

I visit the Aboriginal Sacred Sites Protection Authority. The Authority is a government body whose statutory job is to establish and maintain a register of sacred sites, and to ensure that they're protected. Yes, I'm told, Anzac Hill and Billy Goat Hill and Heavitree Gap are indeed all registered sacred sites. I'm also told that there are no plaques noting their significance to Aborigines because a former Chief Minister of the Northern Territory decreed that there were to be none.

My mouth is parched, I need a beer. At the bar I shout an order for a Foster's Lager. While I wait I eavesdrop on an argument between a tall thin Aussie woman with scorched skin and a curly-haired Canadian with a gold earring in his left ear. The woman is telling him that all of Australia belongs to whites. She says, "Thank God laws have been made to keep the black-fella in his proper place."

The Canadian counters that Aborigines are no different than Canadian Indians. They've been lied to and dispossessed of their lands. They have, he says, turned to alcohol to assuage their sorrow. "You owe them this land and whatever they want. And you, lady, you're absolutely full of shit! Why don't you read your own history? Why don't you learn how awful whites have treated blacks since Captain Cook landed at Botany Bay in 1788?"

The woman sticks her nose into his face and shouts, "History, you ratbag, is irrelevant! All that matters is the present and how *I* feel!"

I pick up my beer and head for an empty chair at a long table occupied by laughing Aborigines. Aborigines? Shouldn't I be training my mind to think Aboriginals? The word Aboriginal strikes me as an adjective, and yet in much of the literature I've picked up here in The Alice, and especially among whites concerned with Aboriginal issues, Aboriginal is frequently used as a noun. What subtle distinction am I missing? Is there something here that's now as clear as that difference between Negro and black in my own mind? No one seems able to explain why I'll sound more sensitive if I use the adjectival form. No one seems able to tell me why I should call these people Aboriginals when they call themselves Aborigines.

Other distinctions are also proving troublesome, revealing, indicative of change, raw nerves. The other day I was talking with a white Aboriginal activist who does consulting work for the Central Land Council, one of the principal organizations involved in making land claims for the Centre's Aborigines. In our discussions I spoke of "part-Aborigines." He corrected me, saying that it was no longer proper to refer to Aboriginals this way.

"What about the term half-caste?"

"No different."

"What do you use to describe those who are the offspring of, say, a European father and a full-blood Aboriginal mother?"

"Either you're an Aboriginal or you're not."

"There is no parallel to, say, Polish-American?"

"No."

"How do Aborigines refer to themselves when their parentage is mixed?"

"As a half-caste."

"Half-caste is a pejorative term among them?"

"I wouldn't say so." He explained that half-caste was a term given to Aborigines by Europeans. They also speak of quarter-caste and octoroons.

I said I understood that terms like half-caste could be seen as judgmental, conjuring up the notion of bastard. "Is there no acceptable descriptive term for those of mixed parentage?"

"I suggest you use the term urban Aboriginal for half-caste."

"But many urban Aborigines do not have mixed parentage."

"Then if that doesn't work for you just call them Aboriginals."

We had come full circle. There was no place to go, but we talked on. I was apprised of other subtleties that aware people incorporate into their grammar, their thinking, their social relationships in the Outback. Aboriginal culture was never Stone

Age or Paleolithic. These terms, I was to understand, were de-
meaning, judgmental, oppression through words. Notwithstanding that Aborigines used stone implements for tools and had the
most rudimentary or primitive technology, it was now appropriate to see their material culture as, well, "just different from
European culture."

We talked about cultural anthropologists gone amuck with
their notion of cultural relativism. We agreed that there were
legitimate moral judgments to make about South American Indian males who beat their wives senseless with clubs or killed
newborn females. We could not agree about similar kinds of issues concerning Australian Aborigines. Nor could we agree on
an adequate term to describe traditional Aboriginal technology.

I would, it seemed, also have to adjust to a rather peculiar way
of knowing who was and was not an Aborigine. "Anyone," I was
told, "who calls himself an Aboriginal and is recognized as such
is Aboriginal." That one has only a small fraction of Aboriginal
blood, has white skin, speaks no Aboriginal language, and
knows nothing of traditional Aboriginal culture is irrelevant.
Apparently, this new way of reformulating an old anthropologi-
cal category got off the ground more than a decade ago when
Aborigines were legally granted full human rights and given
generous welfare concessions to make up for historical injustices. This contemporary definition of an Aborigine was not, I
would discover, a revisionist category that I could afford to ignore. It would allow me, for example, to begin to understand the
mindset of white and part-Aboriginal carpetbaggers from Sydney and Melbourne who come to the Centre and after a brief
residence arrogantly declare themselves spokesmen for people
about whom they know little more than what they have picked
up in a couple of university anthropology courses.

I cross the sandy, perennially dry Todd River and drive north
through one of Alice Springs' many Aboriginal town camps. I
turn a corner and three male adult Aborigines wave. I wave back.
They motion for me to stop.

Before I can park and get out, they're on the passenger side,
one of them motioning for me to roll down the window.

"Boss, you give us a ride to town? We go get my car in the shop. It fixed now. Give us a ride, boss."

I hesitate, then say that I'll be returning in about ten minutes and I'll pick them up.

"Don't forget, boss."

I drive up the dirt road, past a hill of round red boulders on my right and on my left more concrete Aboriginal homes that seem dark, empty, neglected. In front of one porch, on loose dirt, four Aboriginal women are sitting in a loose circle, their legs neatly scissored. Nearby are food wrappers, dozens of empty green and blue beer cans, some clothing, a shoe, a bicycle that looks broken, other garbage; lots of other garbage.

The house where I see the Aboriginal women talking looks substantial, middle class. All the house needs is a little landscaping, paint, repair work to the iron fence, maybe some jacarandas, bougainvillea, oleanders, tamarisks, an oil drum for a garbage can.

I steal another long look at the colorfully clothed women on the ground, and it occurs to me that I'm in the Third World, in Haiti, or on the coast of Colombia or Ecuador.

A young doctor in Alice Springs who has worked with Aborigines once said to me, "You would not believe how bad off they are. These people, their health problems are just not like those of other Australians. It is all very, very depressing." She told me about the unusually high incidence of high blood pressure among the men, the widespread syphilis, the kidney and liver problems, gastrointestinal complications that kill the very young, the high rate of trachoma among the elderly. Not too many years ago the Australian Broadcasting Commission was asked by a federal health official to cancel a film about Aboriginal blindness for fear that it would damage the tourist trade.

The road narrows and the houses disappear. The dirt road worsens. It turns lumpy, pitted, the fringing edges randomly painted with beer cans and two-litre cardboard wine containers, white plastic shopping bags. I continue on because ahead I see a few more homes. I want to see if there are more Aboriginal settlements upriver.

I lurch into an open, grassy clearing, and from the knoll where

I sit, the car idling, I cannot decide whether or not I have the right to go any farther. The road looks passable, and it seems public. It swings to one side of a small single-story brick house surrounded by a veranda. But all around the house and out toward the road are mattresses and blankets, clothes, a peeling refrigerator half buried in grass, tables, wayward chairs, a tattered couch. Thirty or forty Aborigines are standing, sitting in small groups, lying on the ground or on mattresses.

I want to get out of the car and look inside the house, see if it is being used for storage, not as a living space. Because it's too confining and stuffy. Because if you're inside you can't see what's going on among kinsmen, in the larger encampment. Because you need one house for the women and another for the men; each sex has its own space. Because Aborigines aren't fond of a nuclear arrangement. Because their distinctions between day and night spaces are different than that of white men who planned and built this house.

Are these people classified among Australia's homeless? I wonder. The official figure for the country is 40,000. The Aboriginal Development Corporation in Darwin estimates that more than a fifth of the Territory's Aborigines are without proper shelter. The ADC report includes among its homeless those who sleep under trees or corrugated iron sheets. A recent housing survey estimates that 4,000 houses, flats and pensioner units are needed for Aboriginal families, another 300 shelters for tribal groups in remote areas.

As I drive past, they seem to take little notice of me. But I cannot say the same. Fifty yards from the house, I slow down and gaze in amazement, shock, bewilderment. I find it hard to pull my eyes away, and I veer off the road into weeds, nearly get stuck. I get back on the dirt road. I turn and see several men, women and half-dressed children standing in high weeds amid garbage, around a fire, eating pieces of meat with their hands. Everyone's clothes look dusty and dirty, ragged. Their hair is dull, thick as straw, disheveled.

W. J. Sowden, who traveled in the Northern Territory in 1880, had this to say about Aborigines:

Oh, such degraded specimens of humanity!—less manlike
some than a grunting and chattering monkey. . . . I question
where, on the whole, any beings bearing the semblance
of humanity could be found more low-sunk than these.
Physically the men were well-made, though disproportion-
ately light of tibia; but the women were lank and puffy
and distorted, and, for the most part, ugly as the Father
of Mischief.

We are all savages.

I look for an ablution block, knowing that I won't find one—a
well head, a faucet attached to a pipe glued to a cloud in the
sky—and then I remember how they smell.

One day a station owner far to the north of Alice Springs
showed me where I could wash before dinner. He opened a door
and pointed to showers. There were several of them in a huge
concrete slab room. "Go ahead," he said, "there'll be plenty of
time before tea."

"For stockmen in the old days?" I asked.

"My father employed Aborigines for as long as I can remember. I did too until the '60s, before they got too dear. The
blackfellas never used the showers. Not once in my life have I
seen them take one, and I've been out here all my life. I would
give them towels and say, 'Go ahead, use it.' They would ask me
for buckets to wash their clothes. That was all."

A white who worked with Aborigines told me they don't bathe
because traditionally they have not wanted to pollute their precious water holes, which they've needed for drinking.

The modern Aborigine is ripped and torn, his identity mud-
died, partial, seeking a new form: from desert nomads to the
technologically mad present in less than 200 years.

I return to the corner where I'd been asked for a ride. Only one
of the Aborigines who had beckoned me is now standing in front
of the house. I stop and reach over to open the front door on the
passenger side. I give it a hard push. But he goes to the rear door
and tries to open it. I say, "No, get in up here. With me."

"Good boss, good boss," he says. A generous smile covers his face.

I tell him my name, ask him his.

"William," he says. Then he quickly adds, "Okay boss, I remember your name. You good boss for picking me up."

We drive toward town. I ask William where his car is, the name of the garage where it's being fixed.

"I'll show you boss. Plenty time." William points, guides me down one street, then another, until soon I realize that there are no more car dealers and garages in front of us. Either William is taking me the long way around or on a joy ride at my expense.

"A friend's fixing your car, William?"

"No, boss."

"Where's the car I'm taking you to?"

"You see soon, real soon, boss."

"William, I'm not your boss. Please call me Richard, not boss. Okay?"

"Okay, boss," he says, the timbre of his voice unchanged. William grins with his broken and missing teeth, his full, round, scarred cheeks. William, I guess, is somewhere in his late forties, older than me.

We're west of the industrial section of Alice Springs, heading into another of the Aboriginal town camps. Again, all the signs and artifacts of an evolving slum, all of it muted only by the arresting background of burnt reds and deep greens of the nearby MacDonnell Ranges. Million-dollar lots in another culture; here, too, perhaps in two or three decades when a cunning developer decides that there's too much money to be made to allow this land in the shadow of magnificent mountains to remain in Aboriginal hands.

"Where we going?" I ask William.

"We go find my girlfriend. I have to see her short time, okay? She sixteen and real pretty, you like her very much, boss."

It's an Aboriginal custom that older men have their pick of young girls for brides. Younger men can vie for the widows, undesirable older women. Now this mating mechanism of a once polygynous culture is supposedly breaking down, disappearing.

William, it turns out, doesn't know exactly where to find his young girlfriend. We try first one house, then another, then still another. The last one is full of friends who greet William from the veranda. William is confident that his girlfriend is inside. I tell him that I'll wait for him in the car.

William is gone a long time, but I don't mind. I'm fascinated by the two young Aboriginal children playing in the front yard, climbing over and under and inside a gutted Holden that sits inside the fence like a mighty piece of revered sculpture. The junk is less than five yards from the front door.

The children are curious, playful, full of laughter and energy. I latch onto their deep-set eyes, eyes so penetrating they make me self-conscious. I get on my haunches and try to endear myself to one of them. I smile, offer a hand, give a name, ask his. He moves closer, and I reflexively do something I've done dozens of times. I get on my knees and bark like a dog, I purr, I squeal like a pig. I make funny faces and seek his warmth. Two fingers go into a mouth and the cheeks rise. A smile of trust grows on his cherubic black cheeks.

His sister calls. He flees into the darkness of the monumental underbelly of what I'm coming to understand to be one of the most prized possessions in contemporary Aboriginal culture.

When William returns, he informs me that he doesn't know where his girlfriend is. Maybe she's not around here after all, he says. But would I mind taking him to see other friends? Would I, before we leave, like to get a close look at the *Playboy* magazine he got from his friends?

William, I discover, loves slim legs and big tits.

We make three more stops to visit friends before I tell William that I have some errands to run. "Okay, boss," he says. Then William tells me that he'll have no trouble getting home. He'll call a taxi.

Between sixty and seventy percent of the taxi trade in The Alice is generated by the town's Aborigines. They hail taxis to do their shopping, to visit friends, simply to be driven around for an hour or two to visit while the driver waits and is paid for waiting.

Again and again I hear that young Aborigines are no longer

interested in horses and mustering, in station life, which is just about the only life of labor that most of their fathers have known. The major preoccupation of young Aboriginal men today is learning how to repair the carburetor, the transmission, the valves.

One night I am talking with a horse runner who sells his feral catch to abattoirs. He tells me that on one of his very first jobs he went to Haasts Bluff to strike a deal with Aborigines for their horses. When he got around to talking about numbers of animals he might catch and how much money would be involved in a fifty-fifty split, the Aboriginal elders immediately wanted to know how their share of the profits translated into Toyota equivalents.

Today my car's in the repair shop. I feel in the mood for hitchhiking. I stick up my thumb and look north. My eyes land on three hitchhikers, two males and a female. They were at the same spot yesterday when I drove into town. Now the girl in hiking boots and pink tank top is lying in the dirt, her head propped against a backpack. She's holding up a sign that reads ADELAIDE?

Several cars and four-wheel-drive Toyota trucks zoom past me. In one of them I count nine Aborigines in the truck bed, four in the front seat. Finally a truck with a short bed slows, skids on the gravel. The driver honks.

The door's open when I reach him. "G'day," he says. "I'm going into town. Throw your bag in the back."

The floor and the seat are cluttered with tools, rope, cans of oil, rags, a mean-looking crowbar. He's blond, smiling. He has three small silver rings in his left ear.

I ask him if he's lived long in Alice.

"Three years, little more. Reckon I might stay forever."

"Good town to live in?"

"We're bloody ringbarked by the blackfella. Know what that means?"

I nod, sensing that he can only be referring to all the Aboriginal town camps that fringe Alice.

"Bloody ringbarked by the bastards," he says. This time he sounds like he's shouting into a cave. "Ringbarking's what rabbits do to bushes to kill them when they're hungry. Pigs do it good too. Circle a big tree all the way around and it's no time till you're looking at something dead. You know something else? How is Alice gonna grow if we're ringbarked?"

"Let them move in next door," I say.

He hoots, reaches for his cigarettes lying on the seat, offers me one. I refuse. He lights one and says, "Mate, you don't see the meaning of ringbarking. The real life of the town's inside the ring of blackfella fringe camps. That's how I reckon the blackfella's got us by the balls.

" 'Nother thing about Alice. We got too many crazies 'round here. Big ugly sheilas with too much hair under their arms, making protests and putting up signs. Writing all over about nuclear war. Bloody stupid, I reckon. They're not thinking at all. Must be three thousand of those Americans here working at Pine Gap. You send the spies home and this town'll be dead overnight. It'll become a bloody blackfella town. Fair dinkum, it will."

At the busy intersection of Stott Terrace and the Stuart Highway I tell him that I want to get out.

"Thanks for the ride."

"You're an American?"

"That's right."

"You know bloody well what I'm saying then. You got plenty of blackfella problems where you come from."

MUSTERING
THE MEAT

For a couple of weeks now I've been trying to find out how I can get up in the air cheaply to see a piece of the Territory from a couple of hundred yards off the ground. This means a helicopter, and it also means I'll probably have to find someone who musters cattle and has a big heart. I'd gotten hold of a couple of names, but when I called their offices they were out, or too busy, or never returned one of my many calls. Finally, I get hold of Bob Crogan, who I'm told is as good in a whirlybird as they come. He had once worked in the Top End; now he does a large share of the helicopter mustering in the southern half of the Territory. For several years he's occasionally worked on contract with the Conservation Commission of the Northern Territory, ferrying their scientists around on animal inventory counts, dropping to within twenty or thirty yards of harems of wild donkeys and feral horses so they could be shot by Commission sharpshooters or station owners.

Somehow word has gotten to Bob that I wrote a book on feral horses. Bob wants to meet me, talk about chasing horses.

We hit it off. Bob's fascinated with mustering methods used on wild horses by the Bureau of Land Management in Nevada and Wyoming. How many do they push at a time? How close do BLM cowboys get in their helicopters? What kind of traps do they use? I'm equally intrigued by Bob's methods, by the numbers and kinds of wildlife he sees, by stories of life on remote stations. But I've caught Bob at the wrong time of the year. He's got so many pressing mustering jobs within a 300-mile radius of Alice Springs that he's almost forgotten the name of his girl-friend.

But then one morning, as I'm shifting gears in a dream and waiting for the dogs to start yapping, there's a bang on my trailer door. I jump up and, before I can get my eyes open and my pants on, Bob says, "I got a job you gonna find interesting. You ready to go?"

We hear the loud call for help from Peter, who's sitting on his white horse, smoking a cigarette, tending the lead point of the growing mob of shorthorns and droughtmasters. Unc, who mends fences and insures that cattle have enough water in this far southeast corner of the station, turns to me and says, "Get in, mate. Peter reckons we lost some bulls. We'll give 'em a go."

This is going to be some go, I think, as I try to fashion a makeshift seat out of broken springs and a torn piece of foam rubber on the left side of the four-wheel-drive Toyota jeep. No top, no roll bar, no seat belts, a windshield shattered in several places, a steering problem.

An hour earlier I'd driven the jeep out from the stock camp, fifteen kilometers away. The stock camp was set up under a patch of ironwoods and desert oaks within sight of Clare's bore and the stockyards, where the cattle in this late-season muster would be branded and tested for tuberculosis and brucellosis before being sold to a buyer from Queensland. Before we left the camp, Unc and I had put two cases of beer in small refrigerators and started up the gasoline engines to get the beer cold. Then Unc said that he was going to drive the truck with the food and kitchen gear. He asked if I thought I could handle the jeep. "It's a little whacky with the steering there, mate," he said.

The steering was so shot I had a hard time keeping the jeep on the dirt track.

Now as we charge cross-country, Unc driving, I wonder what the odds are of bashing a tree or an immovable rock and going through the windshield. I don't sit on the thought long. I concentrate on searching the thick scrub for the three or four bulls that could be anywhere. Holding fast to the dashboard grip handle with one hand, I try to cover Unc's blind side. I point to dead trees, large boulders, old eucalypts and acacias very much alive. I try not to think about all the young witchetty bush and acacia we're rolling over, deforming, killing with the V-shaped tow bar and the black bullbar made of two-inch pipe, both of them more than enough to knock a 2,000-pound bull flat.

With no sign of the bulls, Unc turns to me and throws up his hands, smiles with his bad teeth, pulls down on his dusty, wide-brimmed hat. Before I can find something to say he hits the throttle. We swing abruptly left, the spent steering kicks us around to the right, then Unc charges into a tree-lined alley two tires wire. I imagine the problem before we hit the first tree, so I lean into Unc. We bump shoulders and hug an imaginary line running down the center of the jeep. Without doors there's nothing to protect us from the prickly trees and harsh desert brush that lash and rip at the jeep as Unc's heavy foot propels us along on a surface like deeply rutted ice. We bounce, lurch, jump, dare gravity to loosen its grip—all this recklessness to try to catch up with a couple of mean scrub bulls we've never seen.

Before the helicopter came to central Australia in a big way more than a decade ago, bullcatchers in four-wheel-drive jeeps could make a pretty good living running down what most men on horses would be fools to chase. For roughly half the market value of a bull, bullcatchers would nudge and smash a feral critter into submission, forcing it to join those being herded. If pure force and steel didn't do the job, the bull would be flattened. Then his back legs would be roped together, or a rope lashed around the horns and secured to a tree. Later, the bull would be winched into a truck and taken to an abattoir. If a bull got a reputation for being too nasty and uncooperative or couldn't be handled, it was shot and left for eagles and dingoes.

The helicopter not only solved the problem of expensive labor that came about in the late 1960s when, for the first time, Aborigines were guaranteed a wage equal to that of whites (Previously they had worked for little more than food and tobacco rations and, perhaps, pocket change.), but it also made it easier to control herds and increase station income.

Many stations in the Centre have routinely mustered their cattle two to three times a year, to brand calves and turn off steers and bullocks. Because of the enormous size of Outback stations, an owner and crew mustering on horseback can easily miss ten to fifteen percent of the cattle. It takes up to two weeks to cover on horseback an area covered in two days from a helicopter, and a good chopper pilot misses less than five percent of free-roaming cattle. With a large cow bringing as much as $500 at market, a good pilot can put an additional hundred or so cows in the yard for every thousand head on a station. Stations in this part of the Centre have anywhere from 1,500 to 20,000 cows. Twenty-five percent have more than 10,000. Given these numbers, the high costs of petrol and helicopter rental are a bargain.

After twenty minutes and no sign of the wayward bulls, Unc decides to call it quits. We start back toward the herd being put together by airborne Bob and stockmen on horseback. Before we get very far, Unc spots one of Peter's kids having trouble with an obstinate shorthorn. We zoom over and Unc jumps out of the jeep and drops his weight on the rump of the downed cow. The scruffy kid gets on her shoulder and takes hold of a leg. As he reaches into his pocket to pull out a knife, he mumbles that the cow's been giving him nothing but trouble. He opens the pocket knife and reaches down and cuts a hamstring. He hits a bloated vein. Blood squirts up his arm to his elbow. The blood runs over his shirt and down his forearm like water pouring over a dam. The kid ignores the red flood, cuts the other hamstring.

Unc and the kid jump back from the sweaty mass of anxiety. The kid picks up a long whip, cracks it on her flank, tries to bring her to her feet. The four-year-old rises slowly, then stumbles and crawls into the shade of an old-man gidyea tree. She plops down on her stomach and spreads her legs like a gymnast.

Spittle pours from both sides of the cow's mouth as she takes more punishment from the whip. But she won't budge, and her recalcitrance pays off. The kid gives up, wipes sweat off his brow. "The cunt's running days are gone," he says. He clucks from the corner of his mouth, reaches into a shirt pocket for a pouch of tobacco and paper. Then he says matter-of-factly, "Next year you're on the table."

Bob adroitly sets the Bell 47 down beside the 200-liter drum of high octane Avgas. He runs the hose from the drum into the tank on the right side of the helicopter and cranks the hand pump. The Bell 47 is a voracious consumer of gasoline, but that doesn't much concern Bob when he's mustering. Station owners pay the fuel bill, in addition to his hourly rate of $190. Bob does get preoccupied, however, when he checks the oil and sees that it's low again. Before the one-day mustering operation is finished, he'll have spent $100 of company money on oil. It's nearing the end of a long and busy season; the engine needs a major overhaul.

I fasten my simple lap seatbelt while Bob puts on his earphones and scans the gauges. All except the fuel gauge; it's broken, which doesn't sit well with Unc.

"Bob's good, a bloody efficient bloke in that bird of his," Unc says. "But that gauge sitting on empty all the time scares the piss out of me. I reckon I don't need to be up there when that blade shuts off and that bird drops like a bloody brick house."

In the hour or so that Bob was airborne earlier in the day, he chased and cajoled more than 150 cows into a single mob. Now Peter and his two sons and two hired hands are trying to quiet them down so they can drive them to the yards at Clare's Well. Unc will be mob tail man in the bull-catching jeep, ready to chase anything that breaks for the bush.

Bob squeezes the head on the long stick between his legs, steps on the pedals, and we shoot off at a thirty-degree angle. We knock leaves off several mulgas with our draught, then effortlessly climb a perfectly vertical ladder before tilting full to starboard for a look at the noisy gathering below. I stick my head out of the doorless opening into the hot wind and see Unc with a foot up on the jeep dashboard, a piece of grass hanging from his mouth. Right now Unc's a wing man; he's supposed to be guarding the uneven northern edge of the herd.

We swing around and gain a hundred feet, just enough to catch sight of Peter, son John, and one of the hired hands, a young bright-eyed kid from South Australia who wants to be a jackaroo. All of them are on horseback at critical points around the restless blob of brown. They're leaning on their hornless saddles. Bob decides no one needs his help, so he flips us on our side and waves to Peter, who signals that everything's okay. Then he rights us and we run up the valley at fifty knots toward the low, balding mountains to begin a final sweep for cattle he might have missed earlier.

In search of anything big that moves, we swoop and circle, cant and hover, rise and fall into the clutches of arching gidyea, patchy mulga, coolibah. Every move is calculated to locate cattle trying to avoid a hot iron or the meatworks.

Satisfied that nothing's been missed, Bob turns us around 180 degrees and shoots along a surveyor's line straight for a foliated wall of red mountain. A gallop away from a fatal kiss with hard rock, Bob pops us over a quartzite ridge and my heart yo-yos on a fast string. Then, like a hawk on an undulating thermal, we begin a measured run down a wedge-shaped valley and out onto a plain of familiar shapes and muted colors. I catch sight of a patch of blue mallee, and not far away half a dozen white ghost gums forming an almost perfect circle. Two of the ghost gums have several leafless arms. The dead branches are black as pitch.

On the pebbly brown floor just south of the gums I see the distinct yellow outlines of nine horses stamped in the pudding-brown ground. The impressions are unmistakable, haunting, like the work of some larger-than-life artist who'd lined up a harem of the galloping horses, frozen them in place, reduced them to a single dimension, and then in one diabolical stroke flattened them into the parched earth.

I turn into Bob's ear and shout, "Were you out here when Peter shot the horses?"

He nods. "We tried to clean up the station."

The facts can be found in grey cabinets in the offices of the Conservation Commission of the Northern Territory in Alice Springs.

Between April 29 and May 3, 1986, 1,986 feral horses were shot from Bob's helicopter by sharpshooters from the Conservation Commission. At that time, central Australia was experiencing its worst drought in almost two decades. Pastoral inspectors described Loves Creek Station, where the horses were killed, as they might have others in the Centre: a "disaster."

The Loves Creek shooting brought forth vociferous complaints from Australians for Animals, Animal Liberation, and a wide spectrum of big-city animal protectionists. The incident also prompted a letter of inquiry from Buckingham Palace to the Australian High Commissioner. There were protests from the Royal Equerry in London and from the National Equine Welfare Committee of Great Britain, which represents thirty-two horse-loving organizations in England, Scotland, and Northern Ireland.

Many played loose with facts, with their imaginations, with the technicalities of dying. Sue Arnold, the coordinator of Australians for Animals in Sydney, described the killings, which she didn't witness, as "inhumane and brutal." She called for "scientific evidence" that the horses existed in sufficient numbers to warrant their elimination. There was concern by some that horses were shot in the gut or the spine, that foals were trampled by the scared and fleeing adults. A couple of cases of carelessness, a wayward bullet that dropped or injured a foal, those things that inevitably happen when lots of animals are shot were portrayed as if they happened all the time, were done intentionally. Others complained that the horses hadn't been shot in the front of the head. They said that aerial shooters put the bullet into the top of the head, and this inflicted a slower brain death than if the horses had been shot straight-on from the ground. One animal protection group charged that a Loves Creek horse had suffered immeasurably because it had been shot in the jaw. In fact, the remains of the animal in question were recovered far away, at a place called Pine Creek.

In late 1985 the owner of Loves Creek station, Peter Bloomfield, decided that he wanted to change the status of his lease from term to perpetual. He was told by consultants working for the Conservation Commission and the Department of Lands that because of the poor condition of his range, his application would be looked on more favorably if he got rid of some of his cattle and also did something about his large brumby (feral horse) problem. With three rainless years and 5,600 shorthorns unevenly clumped on 4,000 square kilometers and with far too many feral horses, the feed was gone and water holes had dried up. Horses regularly were found dead around bores and wells. The consultants also concluded that feral horses were the major culprits behind soil erosion in the station's heavily grazed intermontane valleys.

Peter Bloomfield didn't think that he had a brumby problem. "I only have six or seven hundred out there," he said at the time. Then he added that he had a couple of hundred "pensioners," retired stock horses that he wanted left alone. If Peter Bloomfield had really had only a thousand or so horses running loose he might not have been in such bad shape. But Peter Bloomfield, like most pastoralists in the Centre, didn't have a decent idea of how many feral horses he had. He was also blithely ignoring the station's history.

In the early decades of this century the Bloomfields had raised horses for the Indian Remount Program. By the 1930s the family found that buyers for horses came to them infrequently. They concluded, as others did, that "to send a mob of horses down to market is just as likely to end in a debit note as a cheque." Some stations in the Centre were already shooting their horses, taking only manes and tails and leaving the rest of the carcass where the animal was shot.

The Bloomfields finally gave up on the horse business and concentrated on raising cattle. Those horses that had been used as breeding stock were simply ignored and left to fend for themselves. They multiplied, particularly during the rain-rich years of the 1970s. Before the decade was over there were enough around that pet-meat shooters were being invited onto Loves Creek to take as many brumbies as they wanted. They shot those easy to get to on the flats and then, the effort not giving a sufficiently high return, they gave up.

Peter Bloomfield finally went along with the consultants' recommendation, primarily because the Conservation Commission and the Department of Lands agreed to foot the entire bill for eliminating the horses. Part of the Conservation Commission's motive for paying the bill was to show other station owners that it was profitable in the long run to eliminate horses. The CCNT began the effort by taking an aerial census; just over 2,000 horses were counted. Shortly thereafter, Bob's helicopter was rented by the Department of Lands, and the CCNT sent out two sharpshooters and a team of veterinarians to verify that the killings were humane. The veterinarians reported that the horses were shot in either the lung or the heart. Most were overkilled; on average, shooters had used almost three bullets per horse.

The Conservation Commission estimated that its campaign netted 1,600 individuals, or eighty percent of the brumbies on Loves Creek Station. To authenticate the figure for future use, it performed another helicopter census. Instead of counting a mere 400 or so horses as expected, spotters found that more than 1,600 horses still were calling the station home.

No sign of cattle anywhere. Bob returns to the serrated ridge and cuts a right angle across several valleys. Three, four, five of them, and still nothing: no red kangaroos, no feral horses, no cattle. Back and forth we go, checking and rechecking, shaking and bawling when we crash a sharp pressure gradient or get caught in an updraft rocketing off a crystalline mountain wall. I try to make sense of the skimpy growth, the extensive, ravaged sacrifice areas around water, the lower reaches of trees under siege by too many large mouths, the tennis courts of barren, red, stony earth.

From the air I cannot distinguish one grass from another, but it does not matter. I see no measurable hint of the natives: kerosene grass, kangaroo grass, curly windmill grass. Nor do I see evidence of the fifteen or so introduced grasses that reflect the long history of occupation and exploitation of Love's Creek. The "management" scheme here is simple: When forage is present, cattle numbers are pushed up to eat out all the ephemeral growth; when a prolonged dry spell sets in, some of the cattle are sold. But far too many of them are pushed into the hills and less accessible areas to eat anything that resembles feed. As on so many stations in the Centre, management practices are crude, paleolithic, utterly destructive. I once calculated that station owners in the Centre pay their government about sixty cents per year for each square mile they presumptuously call their own.

It's time to have another close look at the dense trees that line the dry riverbed. Up and down we follow the zigzagging course lined with river red gums, here and there a coolibah with its dark corrugated bark. The bleached, sandy riverbottom is full of animal tracks, linear stippling that more or less runs perpendicular to the flow of the river. The crisscrossing lines resemble quilt-stitching in search of geometrical order.

On the first run down the river I see a large ginger dingo prowling just below a family of gum trees. Its snout hugs the ground; it seems oblivious to our presence. On the second pass Bob and I simultaneously spot four shorthorns under a serried line of river red gums. We angle down to within twenty yards of the gathering. The air rushes and swirls, the trees dance, the air clouds; and two heifers immediately get to their feet. Within mere seconds all of them have gotten the message and are walking in the general direction of the main herd that Peter and the others are now pushing toward the stockyards. Not wanting this small batch to meet up with the main mob too soon, Bob pulls back and up.

We continue the downriver search.

When we don't find more cattle we return to the big march and set down on an invisible platform high above the mustering action. Bob sighs, tunes into his radio, then puts his eyes back to work, looking for breakaways, hiders, developing trouble spots. I gaze at the liquid flow, all the marketable beef being reluctantly squeezed like cookie dough through the paddock gate.

Suddenly two shiny brown cows just this side of the gate break loose and begin loping along the barbed wire fence. Peter comes alive, gives his horse a slap, gives chase. One of the cows gets a change of heart and returns to the mob. The other one pulls up short after a brief rumble and snuggles up to the fence. Just as Peter pries her loose and gets her turned around and heading in

the right direction, a white-faced critter on the thinning tail of
the herd makes a dash for heavy scrub. Unc hits the throttle
before she's put twenty yards between her and the others. He
spins an arc, and before the half-ton animal reaches the first
knot of mulgas he's in front of her.

Unc moves in close and revs the engine, tries to persuade the
beefy animal to change her mind. She'll have none of it. He
smashes into the cow's right shoulder. He knocks her to her
knees. Stunned, she falls over and lies motionless on her side.
We're close enough to see her face covered in a soup of dust and
spit. After a long minute the cow gets up and wobbles like a
hopeless drunk. She shakes her head, opens her mouth like a
pair of pliers, peers straight into the bullbar. Unc waits—and
she waits. Then she begins a slow retreat, again heading off in
the wrong direction.

Unc has had enough. He grinds the jeep into reverse, eats up
watery herbs with his grooved tires, signs the ground with a J.
Now he shoots around in front of the lumbering, single-minded
cow and bangs her viciously with the bullbar. Down she goes.
This time she does a shaking roll. Her legs straighten out, salute
the formless pure blue sky. When she finally comes up, she
slumps into a resigned sitting position. Unc moves to within a
foot or so of her face with the bullbar to persuade her to get up.

Bob scans the ground below us for other problems. He decides
to give Unc a hand. We roar down a soft gradient and without
pause Bob puts the skids somewhere between the shattered
windshield and the cow's lowered head. He's close enough to
lean over and slap her a good one with a yardstick. But none of
this is necessary. The deafening fwap and hard clatter of the
frightening flying machine bring the animal to her feet. She
turns and begins a begrudging walk toward the funneling mob.

Twenty-five minutes later a new problem develops. Peter
hasn't found the time to extend some long hessian wings out
from the stockyards. Even short ones would have worked, made
it easy to push the cattle into the yards instead of giving them a
chance to declare a free-for-all rodeo on the scorched earth
around Clare's Well once they became aware of their fate.

For the better part of forty minutes Peter and his sons and Unc and the jackaroos and Bob in his amazing whirlybird work their butts off trying to persuade nine cows and two bulls to enter the yards. One minute Bob brings us down to ground level to cut off a fleeing animal; the next minute he joins up with Unc or one of the jackaroos on horseback to ease the task. Then he spins a large circle around the yards to see if someone's missed a breakaway. Up and down and around and around we go, putting the helicopter mere feet above cows to get them up and moving, touching down and kicking up a storm to cut off a fleeing steer, swinging back and forth at tree level to get an animal to change its mind and head for the yards. One meaty bullock occupies Bob in his helicopter and Unc in his jeep and one of Peter's kids on horseback for better than ten minutes. Finally the bull sits down in the hot sun twenty-five yards from the gate and won't move for anyone.

He's asking for a bullet in the head.

Dan takes off his plastic right arm and tosses it in the back of the tucker wagon like it was a second-hand shovel. Then he goes over to the pile of mulga limbs and kicks several large pieces under the iron grill perched on boulders. He turns to the apprentice jackaroo and says, "Get me that can full of petrol, would'ya kid."

"What?"

"The fucking petrol! There!" He motions with his hand-sized stump toward the tree behind the kid.

The kid smiles meekly. His eyes grow large and dumb, as if Dan had spoken to him in some Bantu language.

Dan shakes his head, wiggles at the kid with his scarred pink stump, spits at his feet, then ambles over to the desert oak and picks up the gas can. He returns to the campfire and with a fast motion yanks the ten-litre can up onto his lap, holds it with his stump and shoulder, and unscrews the cap with his only hand. Then with a trick motion worthy of a magician he begins soaking the wood. Putting down the can, he pulls out a box of matches and lights one. He flicks the match onto the fuel. Ten-foot orange flames consume the grill. Dan grins like he's just won a bundle on a twenty-to-one shot at the racetrack.

On the other side of the desert oak Peter sits down on a steel bedframe. His beer gut rolls onto his thighs like a high wave. He tilts back his hat, forms a fist and wipes the grimy sweat off his brow, around his graying black mustache. Then he lets out a deep sigh, as if to say, *Like what the bloody hell am I doing out here this time of year? These cattle should have been mustered two months ago when it was cooler.*

Presently, Peter fixes his eyes on the four-wheel Toyota motorcycle. Slowly, as if he can't decide whether the effort is worth it, he gets up and shuffles his lopsided frame over to the right rear tire to see that his eyes aren't deceiving him.

"Cunt!" he growls. He shakes his head, searches around in the dirt and dead buckbush for a wrench. He finds nothing and scowls, cusses again, then finally turns to Unc and says, "Can't have a flat like this if we need it to run one down, Unc. Get it fixed."

"No worries there. She'll be right."

Meanwhile, one of Rob's sons, toast-brown and looking thoroughly exhausted, has picked up a steel folding chair. He drags the chair into the shade of the tucker wagon, sits down and drops his head onto his lap. A long minute passes and then he gets up and scrounges around inside a refrigerated box. He comes up with a plastic jug of ice-cold water. He fills a tin cup, takes several gulps, then wets a hand and wipes the back of his neck before throwing what's left on his face. Now he slouches down on the metal chair and spreads his legs wide, as if a nine-minute catnap is a foregone conclusion. His arms drop and his hands come to rest in browning bush buttons and saltbush. The blood on his cowboy shirt has turned black and crusty, pinched the cotton into hard folds.

Others are sitting on their haunches now. They're nursing a cup of water, a cigarette, tired bones, private thoughts. Trying, like me, I think, to ignore the heat. By rough calculations, it's 110 in the shade. There's no breeze.

There are a million hungry flies that love humans.

Neither the heat nor the pesty flies seems to concern Dan.
He's taken ten steaks cut for Sumo wrestlers out of a cooler.
He's spreading them helter-skelter on the grill. He fills a large
square lard tin with water, places it to one side of the steaks,
and drops in two heaping handfuls of tea. Returning to the
tucker truck, he tears open a loaf of white bread with his teeth
and takes out a jar of hot peppers, a bottle of tomato sauce. He
puts them beside the bread and then leans against the truck to
enjoy a cigarette. The cook's done for this meal. Steaks, bread,
peppers, tomato sauce, tea. Mate, that's all there's gonna be for
eight hungry men.

No one says "Time to eat" or "Now." No one says "You better
grab one before it turns to charcoal." When the urge grabs hold,
Peter or Bob or Unc or the apprentice jackaroo slowly gets up
and grabs a steak and sticks it between two slices of bread. Several of them eat the thick fat around the overdone meat as if it
were a favored entree. Dan peels off the fat with his teeth and
drops it between his feet. He calls a black and tan mongrel pup
to come get his share of the midday tucker.

Tea, cigarettes, and a basketful of short stories later, John says
there's one small bunch of cattle hiding in a valley a couple of
miles west of the stock camp. "Shouldn't take more than three
of us to get them," John says. It doesn't. Bob in the helicopter,
Unc in the bullcatching jeep, and Dan—once he's strapped his
artificial arm to his shoulder and tied it to the handlebar—on
the two-wheel Yamaha dirt bike.

Forty-five minutes later the job is done. The muster, it's
agreed, was pretty clean. Only one cow was lost. "She was running hard and then just goddamn stopped," John says. "I went
up to her and she was lying there. Fucking dead. Reckon she
couldn't take a little heat."

THE HORSES
MUST BE KILLED

Along a charming creek that winds its way north out of Finke
Gorge National Park in central Australia hikers came upon
horrifying, nauseating scenes. Scattered along a five-kilometer
stretch of Ellery Creek were more than 120 brumby carcasses.
The horses had died of starvation. Others, bony and staggering,
were searching for water and anything that resembled feed, of
which there was precious little.

The Conservation Commission had done what it could to
stave off the tragedy. It had permitted feral horses and cattle on
an adjoining station to use a permanent water hole in the park.
It had done so because the station owner was not providing
water for the animals; to his way of thinking, it was easier and
cheaper to use what belonged to the government. The Commission could have told the station owner to put up a fence and
keep his cattle and the horses out of the park, but it didn't. It
saw itself faced with a sticky issue. If the horses and cattle
weren't allowed in, they might die from starvation or lack of
water; if they were, they would eventually destroy the vegetation. They could also do considerable damage to the water hole,
which was frequented by spinifex pigeons, crested pigeons,
honeyeaters, zebra finches, wedge-tailed eagles, rock wallabies,
euros, dingoes, and fish unique to the Centre. People on vacation also sought out the water hole for swimming and picnick-
ing, and for the pleasure of seeing the horses. Which complicated the Commission's job, because some people, upon hearing

a rumor that the Commission was about to build a fence on one side of the water hole, complained that the horses wouldn't be able to drink. Finally, in November of 1985, damage in the park by then clearly evident, the Commission found the courage to tell the offending pastoralist to muster both cattle and horses. He didn't, so the Commission put up a fence and hoped that the station owner would find his conscience. He did not.

At about the same time as the Ellery Creek dieoff, two scientists from Alice Springs took a thirteen-day hike through the MacDonnell Ranges, from Mt. Zeil, the highest mountain west of the Great Divide, to Alice Springs. Trekking where people seldom go, the venturesome pair came upon a score of relict species of plants and animals. One of the keen-eyed scientists, Graham Griffin, concluded that feral horses were having a devastating impact in the MacDonnell Ranges.

"Plants were grazed right down and trampling had finished off most of them," he said. "We saw the area at the end of a dry period. The horses had eaten all the food in the area and were consequently dying in huge numbers."

When the Conservation Commission did systematic aerial censuses of feral horses in the Northern Territory for the first time in the early to mid 1980s it came up with a figure of 238,000. Less than a decade earlier, an American academic geographer, Tom McKnight, sent questionnaires to the Territory's pastoralists. Based on responses, he estimated there were between 40,000 and 60,000.

Government land managers and conservationists gave much greater credence to McKnight's estimate than they should have. Pastoralists invariably have many more animals on their stations than they claim, and not just because they want to minimize their tax debts or avoid hassles with government extension agents. The average station encompasses more than 3,500 square kilometers. Cattle and horses alike are elusive on such extensive properties, and cattlemen make little effort to tally livestock, to say nothing of animals they do not systematically muster. Furthermore, when asked by the government or outsiders, pastoralists are prone to purposely underestimate livestock numbers, especially of brumbies. A high figure, they reason, makes them appear to be inefficient managers who abuse the land.

The current estimate of 238,000 feral horses, which is based on horses actually seen, doubtless is below the true figure. Virtually everywhere in the world, scientific censuses underestimate the abundance of large mammals.

Even 100,000 brumbies are far too many hard-hoofed heavy animals for the land's lean carrying capacity, especially considering that the animals concentrate on the best land and ignore spinifex desert. Spinifex is a perennial, drought-resistant grass that is unpalatable to livestock. There are more than 220,000 square miles of spinifex in the Territory, roughly half its total area.

If there were 300,000 feral horses and they were equally distributed on land with palatable grasses, then there would be about one horse for every square mile. Few places in the Territory free of spinifex can support more than this number, to say nothing of also giving sustenance to a million head of livestock and millions of native wild animals. This kind of calculation is seldom made by people accustomed to measuring the carrying capacity of land by the norms of Great Britain or the American Midwest, where rich soils, ample rain, and lush green pastures mean that a dozen or more horses can be fed in a square mile. People using these Northern Hemisphere norms, ignorant of how much of the Centre's land has palatable grasses and equally ignorant of the needs of native flora and fauna—and livestock, which for historical and social reasons cannot be easily removed—erroneously conclude that the Northern Territory can easily support a million or more feral horses.

Even the kind of straightforward calculation just discussed, however, actually paints too bright a picture. As the aerial surveys of the Conservation Commission show, and as those who know the whereabouts of brumbies will attest, reality is much more sobering. Feral horses are, in fact, highly concentrated in two areas: where cattle predominate and in mountain ranges inaccessible to cattle. Where there are both horses and cattle, it's a truism to say that there's overstocking. It's a truism because even where there are no horses—only cattle—grasses and native wildlife are battered and threatened. In the mountain ranges, which are inhospitable or inaccessible to cattle, virtually all damage done to native flora and fauna can be attributed to feral horses.

The horses are having a traumatic effect on precisely those remote and inaccessible areas that hikers and nature lovers so prize for their pristine habitats and native animals. The horses consume remote mountain water holes and despoil others with their dung. Because rivers and creeks rarely have running water in them, they seldom get flushed and are therefore easily polluted. The horses also deplete food and destroy cover so necessary to native wildlife. So it must be concluded that whatever measures are taken where both feral horses and cattle share grasses, the horses must be eliminated from remote high mountains. It's not just that these are among the most beautiful landscapes in the Territory, but also that these are the last refuges of threatened and endangered native species.

Prior to the introduction of hard-hoofed animals into Australia the native fauna had little detrimental effect on the vegetation. But weighty, hungry animals—too many cattle and too many horses alike—have altered all that. They have significantly reduced the density of vegetation, drastically changed species composition, disturbed root systems, and compacted soil. Overgrazing has exposed the soil to the forces of water and wind erosion, thereby destroying the products of millennia in mere years. Palatable species have been replaced by inedible weeds. The loss of perennial grasses has meant fewer seeds for birds, while a diminished vegetative cover leaves fewer protective canopies for small ground animals.

More than a quarter of the Northern Territory, or more than half the land grazed by introduced animals, requires some sort of mechanical treatment to restore it to a stable condition. This staggering degradation has been caused by pastoralists in fewer than a hundred years, pastoralists who today contribute about ten percent to the economy of the Territory.

Conservationists and scientists familiar with the Centre estimate that more than forty percent of the Territory's native arid-zone mammals have gone extinct since Europeans arrived just over a hundred years ago. Several species of bandicoot, bettongs, a native cat, and wallabies are gone. Virtually no one can find the once abundant and widespread brushtail possum that nested in large termite mounds, limestone sinkholes and hollow trees.

The stick-nest rat is another victim of overgrazing in the Centre. A rather large rat-sized rodent, it was widely distributed throughout much of arid and semi-arid Australia when Europeans arrived. Numerous early explorers frequently commented on their nests of tightly interwoven sticks up to a meter high. The nests were mistaken for signal fires left by Aborigines. Their conspicuous nests provided them with shelter from extreme temperatures and protection from predators. But they were defenseless against the rabbit invasions, the fox invasions, the pastoral invasions. The greater stick-nest rat last was seen on mainland Australia in the 1920s. Fortunately, a colony of them became established on Franklin Island in the Great Australian Bight. A relative, the lesser stick-rat, was not so lucky. It last was collected at Mount Crombie in northwestern South Australia in 1933.

Between 1981 and 1984 the Conservation Commission, in conjunction with cattlemen, shot tens of thousands of feral donkeys, principally in the northern half of the Territory. There was no market for live donkeys, and only an unreliable one for pet meat. Though less than half the size of a brumby, a feral donkey can be almost as destructive of vegetation.

By 1986, concerned that cattlemen were doing nothing to further eliminate or keep their feral donkey populations under control, the Conservation Commission sent scores of them individualized fliers. The one addressed to the manager of Auvergne station was typical.

    1. Before the Conservation Commission started shooting in 1981, your station contained about 1,960 donkeys.

    2. The Conservation Commission shot 1,232 donkeys on your station between 1981 and 1984.

3. There were about 1,580 donkeys left on your station after shooting finished in 1984.

4. If you have kept the number of donkeys down to the levels left in 1984, continue to shoot at least 450 donkeys each year.

5. If you haven't shot many donkeys since 1984 you probably have around 1,900 on your station now. If you think that the current numbers are acceptable for your station, shoot 470 donkeys each year.

6. If you haven't shot many donkeys since 1984 but you want to reduce numbers to 1984 levels within three years, shoot 570 donkeys for three years. After three years you will only have to shoot 450 donkeys each year.

7. If you want to be up to your arse in donkeys within three years, don't shoot any donkeys.

For sixty kilometers east of the Stuart Highway we bumped and rolled through impressive patches of ironwood, mulga, corkwood, gidya, magnificent fields of native fuchsias. I'd lost count of the galahs and little corellas and budgerigars we'd seen. Finally, sleepy-eyed Dave Berman turned to me and suggested that we have something to eat before getting to The Garden homestead. Dave often stops to have a yarn and a beer with Jim Turner, the station owner, but he hates to impose or to arrive too close to lunch.

A doctoral student at New England University in Armidale, New South Wales, Dave frequently comes out to The Garden station to collect data for his dissertation on the ecology and behavior of feral horses. He spends his time observing the horses and making transect counts of dung to measure their numbers and movements. Dave chose to work on The Garden because of the large number of brumbies there and the diversity of environments: riverine, plains, low and rugged hills, mulga with perennial grasses.

Earlier on the drive into the station we had stopped on a scruffy hillock to look at grasses that brumbies relish. After Dave handed me clumps of oat grass, kerosene grass, and five-

minute grass, all of which horses love to nip low to the ground,
I asked him where the horses go when they run out of good feed.

He pointed to Mt. Johnstone and to the mountains to the east.
"You'll find them up there when it gets dry and flogged out
down here. Up there they'll go after the kangaroo grass."

"What's your estimate of the number of brumbies on the station?" I asked.

"Three thousand anyway. Could be four thousand. Somewhere in that range. Hard to be sure, but there's a lot around and
they love to eat."

The figures Dave gave me for feral horses on the station were
close to the number of shorthorns Turner ran.

During Dave's two-and-a-half-year study of horses he's found
that they range out farther from water than cattle do in foraging
for food. Not only do they eat plants and grasses that cattle often
do not get to, but they also skim off the best feed first. Where
horses are abundant, there are few red kangaroos, few euros, few
song larks, few pipits, few quail, few granivorous birds.

I asked Dave if Jim Turner had made any effort to get rid of his
horses. Dave said that the previous year he'd helped Turner muster 300 brumbies that were subsequently sold, half to the abattoir in Tennant Creek and the other half to the competing plant
in Peterborough, South Australia. The abattoir in Tennant Creek
was so desperate to get Turner's horses that it was willing to
pick them up on the property, pay the freight bill, and still pay
a tidy sum for the animals. Many of Turner's horses were full of
Clydesdale genes. Big, meaty horses bring a larger per-pound
profit in the abattoir.

Turner, Dave went on, would get rid of some of his horses if
he had to, but he'd only shoot them as a desperate last resort. He
didn't want to see the meat wasted. The need to get rid of the
horses had become critical in the last eighteen months, since
there had been little or no rain. The effect of no rain had become
particularly noticeable the last six months. Horses were dying
at water holes, and you could just about count their ribs while
sitting in your four-wheel-drive truck.

"The animal protectionists gave Jim a real go for getting rid of
them," Dave said. "There for a while he was getting fifty to

sixty angry letters a week. One of the protectionists from Darwin who was mad about the horses going for food called Jim. Jim told the bloke, 'You want some of them, come down. You can have them for free. Any of them you want. I'll even help you pick them out.' "

Horse lovers said that The Garden station brumbies were descended from horses of the famous Australian Lighthorse Corps, which had distinguished itself in the Boer War and World War I. Known as walers because the first ones had come from New South Wales, the Lighthorse Corps mounts were a cross between a draft horse and a thoroughbred. They were bred for endurance and temperament.

Some of the heavier stock whose genes would later appear in the Australian Lighthorse Corps were brought to the Centre in the 1870s for construction work on the Overland Telegraph Line and in the mines around Alice Springs. By the 1880s the horses were being sold to the British army in India for its flourishing remount program. There they were used for cavalry mounts, as gentlemen's hacks, as race and carriage horses, as chargers. They also were popular with Indian princes and rajahs, who bought them for their private cavalry units. In the 1890s, 5,000 horses a year were exported from Australia. Between 1899 and 1902 more than 16,000 were shipped to South Africa for the Boer War. Eight times this number were used on the battlefields of World War I.

The Turners actually had two markets for their horses; smaller stock was sold to the British for the Indian army and larger horses went for hauling wagons. When The Garden station stopped selling horses to the British in 1938 (the remount program came to an end in 1946), it was believed to have the largest single stock of walers anywhere in Australia. Along with Loves Creek, The Garden and a few other stations north and south of Alice Springs were renowned as "the horse stations."

As Dave opens a can of runny cold spaghetti that we'll pour onto some white bread and call lunch, he begins musing about what he's going to do when he finishes his degree. "Reckon if I could find the capital to get started, I'd go into the brumby-mustering business," he says. "Lot of money to be made there if you do it right."

Dave and I go through a long list of ifs and buts. We wonder how much work would be required to block off enough water holes so that horses could be trapped in yards rather than chased in expensive helicopters. We talk about ways to get station owners to agree to let us trap their horses. We imagine how much of the profit they'll demand. Then Dave returns to the nagging question of how a broke graduate student is going to acquire the capital needed for trucks and trap panels and living expenses while he's getting the horse-running business off the ground.

"But why don't the station owners muster the horses themselves?" I ask.

Dave shakes his head as if he's got enough to think about with more than a hundred plants to be identified and his dissertation still to be written. He circles the can of spaghetti with a hand to get rid of the horde of flies and offers me another pour.

Jim Turner greets us outside the front gate. He's wearing dark blue work pants and a matching shirt. His gray hair is disheveled. His eyes have a tired, sad, watery look. He has the reddish, lined face of someone who's spent too much time in the harsh sun.

He invites us in for tea and biscuits, to meet his wife. We get no farther than the kitchen and a long wooden table. The kitchen is dark and needs paint, repair work. The stove seems like a relic out of the 1940s. I can't quite make a connection between any of this and a few facts I'd picked up about Jim Turner before coming. He's alleged to be a millionaire, and not merely in the paper sense. His grandfather and his father not only made The Garden prosper, they also made a fortune buying and developing what is now Alice Springs' central business district. Where, then, is the extravagance in Jim Turner's life? In the horse races he's addicted to? In the heavy gambling he did at the casino in Alice Springs the first couple of years it was open? Or is Jim Turner simply another one of those rich oddballs who has more interest in numbers on bank statements than in how he lives?

I want to talk about all the feral horses on his property and what he might do about them. I'd heard from people in the Conservation Commission that Jim Turner loves horses, and that whatever else happens in the Territory he's not going to let those on The Garden be shot or removed without a fight. I'd learned that he might be persuaded to sell more to the abattoir, but that it wouldn't be easy getting him to give up large numbers. He won't even listen to his son, who's anxious to get rid of all of them. His son wants the feed brumbies are eating turned into marketable beef.

The conversation moves in fits and starts, like a car with a serious carburetor problem. At one point Dave mentions that I've written a book on feral horses in the U.S. Detecting a glimmer of interest in Turner, anxious to hear how he sees the horses, I run through some of the highlights of federal legislation protecting them. Then I get on to some specifics: names, dates, a story about one rancher and the disastrous changes to his rangeland when he found himself with too many wild horses. "He'd long had a profitable operation, but slowly the horses began driving him toward bankruptcy," I say.

Turner yawns, asks if I'd like some more tea. I nod, and he tells me to help myself to the tin of cookies.

"You've got some gorgeous country here," I say, trying to come at him from a different direction. "On the way in, we saw some huge flocks of cockatiels and budgies, larger than anything I've seen since I've come. It'd be a pity to lose them."

"It's the recent rain."

Then we get to talking about birds, finches, vast flocks of zebra finches he's had on the station in past years.

"Don't know what's happened to them this year and the last couple," Jim Turner says. "You could find their nests all over. In the shed, in the eaves. . . . I've had so many drown at bores in past years I didn't know how I would get them all out."

We never do return to horses.

Until after World War II, the only water available to cattlemen was found in rock holes and here and there in an occasionally wet river or from wells. The wells were dug near rivers, in sinks, where it was known with near certainty that flowing water would be found without too much backbreaking shovel work. When natural sources of water dried up in a drought the cattle were brought into a well. Then when the well went dry, as it often did in a real drought, the pastoralist simply stood by and watched his cattle perish. On some stations thousands would die at a single well. Because overstocking of livestock was as commonplace a hundred years ago as it is today, all of the good country near semi-permanent water and wells was badly overgrazed. After World War II, and especially in the 1950s and 1960s, scientists learned how to find water far from obvious places, and how to get it out of sandstone. Cattlemen began to sink bores wherever there was good feed that previously was unavailable to their cattle. This new phase of mining the land altered the calculus of destruction immensely. Now everything that cattle could reach within a day's walk from a bore site was subject to immediate change: perennials to annuals, native grasses to woody shrubs, rich soil to hardpan and gravel, bird and small mammal life to flight and nesting elsewhere—or extinction.

What was good for cattle was even better for feral horses, for they're willing to walk much farther to water in a day than cattle are—twice as far, maybe farther. Horses not only could multiply by finishing off vegetation that cattle might first have gotten to, but they could also enjoy grasses not reached by cattle. One might wish that it were the other way around. The dentition of cattle is not nearly so efficient as that of horses, and cattle do less damage to plants.

New water, of course, also increased the numbers and the range of red kangaroos and euros in arid Australia. This, no doubt, gladdened the hearts of many. But real joy was short-lived. Too many cattle and too many feral horses have seen to that.

One scientist with the Commonwealth Scientific and Industrial Research Organization (CSIRO) in Alice Springs told me that twenty years ago you'd see eighty to a hundred red kangaroos on the road in the first twenty-five kilometers north of Alice Springs, and this wasn't counting how many you'd see off the road. Now you're lucky to see one or two over the same stretch of highway, and you won't see that many unless you're straining to find them.

What's behind the reluctance of pastoralists to dispose of their brumbies?

1. Station owners have grown up with horses and they're attached to them. Many are smitten with the romance of walers, and, like so many Australians, can't stay away from rodeos and racetracks.

2. Like them or not, pastoralists usually don't see enough commercial value in brumbies to go to the trouble of setting water traps or hiring a helicopter pilot or inviting someone on to their station to muster the horses for a share of the income. They can make a profit, but it's not enough, given the marginal return and their feelings about the horses.

3. Some station owners have a pretty good understanding of how much feed the horses are taking and the fence damage they cause. But historically they've been attuned to putting the brunt of their problems on other scapegoats: lack of rainfall, floods, fire, falling market prices, the government, kangaroos, rabbits, dingoes. Pastoralists prefer to throw their time and money at issues that are palpable, immediately measurable. Better than ninety percent of the station owners take measures to control dingoes, but less than a quarter do anything about feral horses. If they'd don an accountant's visor for a long moment, they'd see that the horses are costing them a great deal more than dingoes in lost feed, in damaged range, in broken fences.

Then you've got other reasons that pertain to a smaller class of pastoralists. For one, you've got station owners who just aren't aware of the damage the brumbies do. They see the broken fences and they see the horses at the dams drinking all the time, but they never work out in their minds how much the horses cost them.

Others don't like government interference. If a proposal to do this or that with brumbies originates in a government agency, then something must be wrong with it. Many station owners have lived in the Centre all their lives, and one of the first things they ask of government people is: How long have you been here?

They know the answer in advance, and they always react with the same all-knowing cockiness.

Some of them will get rid of their horses when they're out there in high density. But then they start thinking just like rabbit and dingo shooters. They want to keep a good thing going, so they only get rid of so many. Then there's the other side of the problem. When they've got horses in low densities it doesn't look profitable to do anything, so they don't.

Then take the case of the cattleman who has a serious problem with brumbies knocking down fences. Problem is, the fence is a boundary between stations and both stations have feral horses. One guy wants to get rid of the horses, but the other one's indifferent or he figures he'll "get to it someday." If a boundary is shared with a national park, the government may or may not be willing to assist when the pastoralist has the time and money to go after the horses. So in the end the responsible pastoralist calculates the high cost of hiring a helicopter and the lack of cooperation from neighbors and so decides against it.

Aboriginal lands pose a somewhat different problem. Most have lots of brumbies, and while Aboriginal leaders may want to sell them or share in the profits of a muster, they're seldom in a hurry to do so.

For those who love horses, and for those who believe that all life is sacred, there are no easy solutions to the problem of the Territory's feral animals. But no matter what one feels in the heart, hard choices must be made. It must be recognized that, by definition, all feral animals are artificial creations. They are simply domestic animals that have reverted to a wild state. This fact should distinctly color how we rank them. And rank our priorities we must, no matter how distasteful the exercise.

Before considering these priorities, contemplate a simple hypothetical. Assume that all of the Territory's feral horses were eliminated tomorrow. Were this to happen, and were Australians to decide that this was an unacceptable state of affairs, very large and thriving feral horse populations could be reestablished in a mere half-dozen years. All that need be done would be to release large numbers of domestic horses.

Top priority must be given to soils, mere dirt to untrained eyes. There may be nothing sexy or aesthetically moving in contemplating riverine or calcareous soils, but once soil has been lost it can take hundreds or thousands of years to be replaced. Some soils can never be brought back. Without productive soils, there is no plant life, no animal life, no life. Native plants and animals must be next on a list of priorities. Extinction means gone forever, unique life and genetic diversity lost to all future generations.

One possible way of reducing brumby numbers would be to sell them to abattoirs for pet food and for human consumption. But Australians, like Americans, have no taste for horsemeat. In fact, they have a strong cultural aversion to it.

None of the Territory's feral horses south of Tennant Creek— somewhat less than half of the total population—can be sold for pet food. This restriction came about in 1984 when indospicine, a very stable toxin produced by a plant called Birdsville indigo, was identified as the cause of death in more than thirty pet dogs in Alice Springs. Indospicine builds up in tissue and remains in a horse's system for months after it has eaten Birdsville indigo. When meat contaminated by indospicine is fed to dogs it causes liver disease and death. Apparently, the toxin does not affect humans.

Birdsville indigo is a low, spreading forb and one of the most troublesome weeds in central Australia. Along with couch grass, Mossman river grass, and Bathhurst burr, Birdsville indigo is a good indicator of land abuse. Generally, the plant increases after the land is heavily grazed or there has been a prolonged dry period. When other feed is rank or dry, horses actively seek out Birdsville indigo. When they succumb to the disease, they become pitiable. They shiver and shake, they lose their balance and drag their hind legs, they circle and stumble, they sweat easily, and they often rear over backwards. Birdsville indigo is a native plant that cannot be economically eliminated.

There's a notable overseas market for horsemeat for human consumption. At present, Australia has about five percent of the world market, with Japan, Belgium, Luxembourg, and the Netherlands accounting for ninety percent of Australia's total sales. Despite Australia's small share of the world market, its prospect for selling large numbers of feral horses is not good. Both price and demand have declined every year since 1980. Furthermore, Japan, which takes more than two-thirds of Australia's horsemeat in frozen, boneless form, increasingly is substituting beef and pork.

Currently there are only two abattoirs to which Territory pastoralists can send brumbies. One is in Tennant Creek, the other in Peterborough, South Australia. Their present combined capacity for horses from the Territory is 25,000 animals a year, which is less than the current increment of the feral horse population. If it were only a question of abattoir expansion to reduce the brumby population, the issue might be resolved in a way that did not waste valuable protein. But pastoralists, like other businessmen, continually scrutinize the economics of their efforts.

When prices for horsemeat are high and it appears that brumbies can be economically mustered with a helicopter, some station owners will attempt to remove them. But even when the market is good, it often is not economical to muster more than a small percentage of the horses on a station. Brumbies usually concentrate in small numbers in scattered pockets and in rough terrain, factors that dramatically increase mustering costs. Rough terrain or not, feral horses are more unpredictable than cattle and harder to get into a yard.

Frequently a pastoralist will make one or two unsuccessful attempts to muster brumbies and then give up. Some pastoralists can trap horses at water, but many cannot. There often are too many sources of water to control. And if water-trapping is not done with considerable expertise, the exercise can be both costly and futile.

If the magnitude of the problem is to be significantly lessened, another approach must be used. Regrettably, the horses must be killed where they're found in very significant numbers; to simplify a complex biological process, it is largely the base population that controls additions to the population. Shoot as many horses as economically and humanely possible now, and not only will the subsequent costs of control be much smaller, but the positive returns to the environment will be substantial.

There may be other payoffs. All of the Territory's feral animals are either actual or potential carriers of diseases that could have disastrous effects on Australia's livestock and horse-racing industries. African Horsesickness, Glanders, Equine Influenza, Equine Viral Arteritis, and Equine Viral Encephalomyelitis are among the exotic diseases that could be transmitted to domestic horses.

No less important is the possibility of a single diseased animal escaping into areas with disease-free cattle. Feral horses are notorious for damaging fences, which is of particular concern in the Centre, where millions of dollars have been spent to control brucellosis and tuberculosis through the requirement that properties be fenced and livestock routinely tested for disease.

Feral horses should be shot from helicopters. A pilot can follow horses virtually anywhere, and a trained marksman has ample time to shoot at close range and ensure that all brumbies in each group are destroyed. It is neither efficient nor as humane to shoot horses from the ground. Many horses simply are impossible to reach except by helicopter. This is especially true in the lower half of the Territory, where rugged terrain restricts vehicle access. Even those horses that can be approached on foot, on horseback, or in a vehicle will be shot at a distance many times greater than when shot from a helicopter. It is also difficult to get a good second shot at a wounded horse from the ground, and there is a greater likelihood of a foal being orphaned and left to starve to death.

Ideally, horses should be shot during a drought or toward the end of a long dry season. At that time many watering holes are dry and horses concentrate around the few available waters. No other time is as cost-efficient.

This line of reasoning does not sit well with many pastoralists, nor with those concerned with animal welfare. Horses are under stress during a drought. A few may die from exhaustion when pursued by a helicopter. Animal liberationists will be quick to note this as a possibility, adding that dying from stress is not the fastest way to go. The pastoralist, on the other hand, resists getting rid of horses during a drought because it is then that he feels least secure about his future income, which depends on always unpredictable rain. Often, however, it is equally difficult to convince the pastoralist to get rid of brumbies when good rains have brought forth ample grass. Then there appears to be plenty of feed for everything, and the horses, it is reasoned, are not a problem worth worrying about.

Both the animal liberationist and the pastoralist suffer from myopic vision. Surely, it is better for a few rather than many animals to suffer. A few horses dying from stress rather than a bullet is, in the harsh calculus of life and death, more humane than permitting hundreds slowly to starve to death. In starving to death, horses will eat manes and tails, the remains of their own, their own excrement. The excruciating final stages of death by starvation can take several days.

Scarce money spent by a pastoralist when he is preoccupied with weather forecasts and bank loans will give much more than an average return in the long run: more feed for cattle, more nutritious grasses, heavier cattle, a higher turn-off rate, and a longer interval before it is again necessary to muster or shoot horses. Best of all, the pastoralist may be making a positive step away from the pervasive attitude that public land is an inexhaustible resource to be mined until dead.

The experience in the United States may be of help in predicting what may happen if drastic measures are not taken in the near future. Today there are more than 50,000 feral horses in the desert portions of eight western states. Even though this number is only a fraction of those in the Territory, there are many conservationists and range managers in the U.S. who feel that half this number would be more than enough.

Since well before the turn of the century, many ranchers have wanted to keep wild horses on their spreads. They were an extra source of income; to augment profits, some were crossed with Belgians and Percherons or good station studs. A few ranchers saw genuine range value in the horses. They dispersed seeds and kept water holes open in winter for cattle. Some ranchers even took aesthetic pleasure in the horses. But in dry years or when range forage seemed thin or the horses too plentiful, livestock took precedence. Then it was time to get permission from a county commissioner to muster or shoot them. The ranchers would collect bounty at two dollars for a pair of ears or send them to war fronts, to rodeos for bucking stock, to the corral for breaking and ranch use, to abattoirs to be converted to hides and pet food and chicken feed in the U.S. or to meat for human consumption in Japan or Western Europe.

By 1900 it was alleged that there were more than a million feral horses in the American West. They were in demand during the Boer War and World War I. Strong demand began in the early 1920s, when chicken feed processors in California began buying them by the railroad carload. Soon thereafter the Chappel Brothers of Rockford, Illinois, came up with the idea that pet dogs and cats needed a more balanced diet, meaning more protein. By 1935 scores of companies in the U.S. were producing dog and cat food made from horsemeat. Within a decade the slaughter of horses—to be sure, not all of them wild—had risen from 150,000 pounds a year to a high of 30 million. Europeans—Germans, French, Belgians, Dutch—also were buying millions of pounds of horsemeat at this time. They liked it cured, chopped, smoked, as steaks, in sausages. Americans were not similarly inclined.

Feral horse herds continued to decrease in size and number and areal extent, and by the 1950s there were murmurs, then shouts that something had to be done lest wild horses disappear completely from the American West. By the late 1960s it was asserted that there were no more than 20,000 feral horses left on public lands. In fact, there were probably at least half again as many. Whatever the facts, the crusade was on to save America's wild horses, a crusade led primarily by a diminutive, polio-stricken woman with a fanatic's vision.

Velma Johnston was her real name, but to western ranchers, conservationists, legislators, and horse-lovers everywhere she was known as Wild Horse Annie. Mrs. Johnston became involved in the feral horse issue in 1950 when she saw a truckload of gun-maimed horses on their way to an abattoir near Reno, Nevada. She complained to the Bureau of Land Management, but to her chagrin discovered that this presumed enforcer of the

1934 Taylor Grazing Act (legislation designed to ensure more prudent use of rangelands) was at best indifferent, at worst in cahoots with ranchers and horse runners who saw the feral animals as pests, voracious consumers of scarce water and grasses that "belonged" to cattle and sheep. Unsettled by the thought that feral horses were too often poorly treated in mustering operations, Annie began a campaign to halt roundups on public lands.

Largely through Wild Horse Annie's efforts, her home state of Nevada passed a law that made it illegal to chase feral horses with an airplane or helicopter on public lands. Thereafter she worked to get similar legislation passed for all public lands in the U.S. She testified before a U.S. Congressional committee, claiming that whereas there were once more than a million feral horses in the West, that number had been reduced to fewer than 50,000 by the mid 1950s. She asserted that the horses were in imminent danger of extinction. In 1959 the U.S. Congress listened to Annie and made it a felony to use airplanes and motorized vehicles for mustering feral horses on any public land.

By the late 1960s there was so much national support for Wild Horse Annie's cause (only the war in Vietnam was generating more letters to Washington legislators) that fifty bills were prepared by U.S. Congressmen to enact sweeping legislation on behalf of the horses. The cause seemed more pressing than ever; Wild Horse Annie said that only 17,000 feral horses remained.

Her alarm call was heeded, and on December 15, 1971, without a dissenting vote in either house of Congress, President Richard Nixon signed the Wild Free-Roaming Horse and Burro Act into law. The U.S. Congress declared that "Wild and free-roaming horses and burros are living symbols of the historic and pioneer spirit of the West. They contribute to the diversity of life forms within the Nation and enrich the lives of the American people. Furthermore, horses and burros are quickly disappearing from the American scene." Congress made it the job of the Department of Interior, and specifically that of the Bureau of Land Management, to act as custodian for the animals.

After the BLM took control of feral horses in 1971, it soon became evident that there were more of them on public lands than Wild Horse Annie and her supporters had guessed. It also became apparent that left to the procreative dictates of natural selection and without interference by man, they multiplied at amazingly high rates. With the horses now a potential threat to ranching and the brittle desert, ranchers and conservationists began to highlight environmentally destructive horse habits.

It was not long before ranchers began demanding that the BLM either remove all horses or reduce herd numbers to what they had been prior to enactment of the federal law. The BLM more or less tried to do what it could. It mustered thousands of horses, and in the mid 1970s it set up a national adoption program to find homes for the animals. Virtually anyone with an acre or two and a pile of timber for a fence and a romantic hankering for a piece of the American West could adopt a feral horse for a minimal fee. Over the years the price has ranged between twenty-five and two hundred dollars. Until widespread abuse was brought to the attention of the government, individuals could literally take dozens of the horses and pretty much do what they wanted with them. By the late 1980s the BLM had found homes for more than 80,000 feral horses.

But try as it might, the BLM couldn't satisfy the clamoring demands of profit-minded ranchers. The agency didn't have the resources, it didn't have a fund of expertise on which to draw, and it began having trouble getting rid of many horses; some were too old to break, some too ugly, and markets became saturated. To make matters worse, the BLM found itself bombarded with threats and lawsuits from all sides. Ranchers complained that there were too many horses on their ranches and they had to be removed. Protectionists and some conservationists sued to stop mustering. They were certain that the horses were again threatened with extinction.

Chief among groups that have brought numerous lawsuits against the BLM to prevent wild-horse roundups is the American Horse Protection Association. Over the years the AHPA has charged mismanagement by the BLM and cruel treatment of

the horses. The organization has claimed that the BLM consistently overstates the true numbers of feral horses in the West,
ignoring the fact that the BLM has long used actual counts and
rarely updates censuses, and that until recently it paid no attention to yearly increases in the population.

The Sierra Club, the largest and most important conservation
group in the U.S., has been a reluctant participant in the feral
horse issue. Afraid to polarize its diverse membership, many of
whom would side with groups like AHPA, and unwilling to recognize the wild horse as true wildlife, the Sierra Club has left it
up to a few of its western chapter members to formulate local
policies on the horses. Chapter members in Nevada, the state
with the most horses, have come out in favor of reducing horse
herds to numbers compatible with a diverse and healthy ecosys-
tem. A few of its more vocal and active members, however, have
been insistent that the horses be used as a pawn to correct historical abuses of public lands by the BLM and ranchers. They
have wanted to "trade" horses for cattle: for each horse removed, remove a cow or a steer.

On the surface, the argument is attractive. Desertification of
western rangelands is widespread, similar to that occurring in
the Australian Outback. Unfortunately, this hardline trading approach adds to the complexity of an already complex issue, and
it could slow the rate at which horses are removed. The approach has alienated a lot of ranchers and made them less willing to compromise in their demands for removal of the animals
in the interest of a healthier range.

The BLM, in many ways a typical government agency, has not
been nearly as wise as it might have been in managing the
horses. It has done a poor job of completing environmental impact statements on the condition and carrying capacity of western rangelands. Some of those it has completed have been chal-
lenged and shown to be inadequate, which has left the BLM
largely defenseless against rancher claims that their ranges are
not overstocked. The BLM usually has removed horses only
when threatened with lawsuits, so that those ranchers who have
made the most noise have fared best in their demands for horse
removals. Neither has the BLM done a particularly good job of

allocating its resources. Nevada, which has well over half of the nation's feral horses, receives proportionately much less for management of its program.

Activist groups are so strong and vocal that the idea of shooting horses is never even raised. Indeed, the solution I suggest for Outback Australia is unthinkable in the U.S.

Not long after my arrival in the Northern Territory the Conservation Commission asked if I would give a brief talk to its Feral Animal Committee and a select gathering of the Centre's pastoralists on what I'd learned about feral horses in the United States. They had heard that I'd written a book on the subject and thought that an international perspective might throw some light on their own problems. By this time I'd talked to a couple of pastoralists, as well as to Dave Berman and others studying feral horses in the Centre. I had before me census numbers, and I had been told by scientists of the magnitude of the environmental damage the horses were causing.

After outlining the legislative approach to feral horses and something of how they had been managed historically in the U.S., I ventured the thought that once a handful of urban-based horse-lovers in Australia got geared up, they probably would succeed in getting laws passed to maintain very large brumby populations in Australia. Based on the experience in the U.S., these people could not be expected to use rational arguments, to care all that much about the Centre's natural resources, or even to visit the Centre in search of facts. Furthermore, they could easily marshal many more votes in large cities than pastoralists, range managers, and scientists in the Centre could ever hope to garner. If the American experience with wild horses and the Australian experience with kangaroos was any guide, eighty to ninety percent of support for maintaining large brumby populations would come from house-bound women and very young girls, who vote with their hearts. It was, I argued, imperative to take swift and drastic action, to kill as many horses as soon as possible.

"Spare no time and money to get rid of them," I said. I did not try to guess how long the Centre's responsible conservationists and pastoralists had before their best efforts might prove futile in a voting war that would probably take place in Canberra, the national capital. By all measures, Canberra is a world away from the depressing reality of environmental destruction in the Centre.

My presentation was followed by a challenge to the cattlemen in attendance from Ron Hooper, the chairman of the Feral Animal Committee and one of the Commission's most senior members. Ron guessed that the Territory had somewhere between six and ten years remaining before "greenies" from the nation's large cities made themselves heard in the feral horse issue. Then, in his estimation, pastoralists might well find themselves faced with laws similar to those enacted in the U.S. "Then they'd have us," he said.

Ron went on to summarize what the Commission and the Department of Lands had done at Loves Creek, and he drew attention to the fact that it had cost $A6.67 to kill each of the horses.

"We've got about a million dollars over the next five years that we can find for this problem," he said. "We're ready to go shoot horses tomorrow. The Commission will supply the bullets and the shooters, about half the cost. You pastoralists will have to hire the helicopter, the other half of the cost."

Ron Hooper didn't say that the $A6.67 figure was the bargain basement price for killing a horse from a helicopter, that wherever brumbies were found in low densities the cost per horse could be two, three, five times this figure. He didn't say that the cost of eliminating every last horse would be uneconomical by any standards. Nor did he note that a million dollars wouldn't begin to solve the problem, that even if the money were wisely spent and the cost were shared equally with the pastoralists it was probably only enough money to eliminate twenty percent of the Territory's brumbies. But none of this mattered. Not a single cattleman took up the Commission's offer. Not that day or in the days or weeks or months that followed.

OUT BUSH WITH BIRD BIOLOGISTS

I'm several hundred miles southwest of Darwin, an hour west of Timber Creek (population "nominal"—two hotels, two bars, two gas pumps), on a cattle station larger than Los Angeles County. Not far from Timber Creek people catch ten- and twenty-pound barramundi. Handsome bush turkeys like small huggable ostriches strut across endless roads as if they were in a well-protected game preserve. Forever noisy red-tailed black cockatoos crowd the high branches of eucalypts by the dozens. Galahs and not-so-little little corellas fill the sky at dawn and twilight like a scene out of Africa.

On the trip north from Alice Springs I passed millions of pin-nacled termite mounds. Brown and ochre and red, the mounds are two feet, four feet, eight feet tall. Some are more than twice the height of a man. They seem as solid as a block of cement, until you give them a couple of hard kicks at the base and they topple. When broken open they're a maze of galleries and chambers.

The termites are the most prolific of all of Australia's wildlife. There may be millions of workers and pugnacious soldiers in a single city. All of the offspring come from one four-inch queen and one much smaller king. The royal chamber, or the queen's cell, is several inches off the ground. The bulky queen, a sickly white hue from her life without sun, is capable of laying 30,000 eggs a day, 100 million over her lifetime.

Most commonly found in mulga and spinifex, termites live on grass and wood and cellulose—trees, fences, fence posts, crops, discarded paper, leather mustering gear. Whatever isn't digested and broken down by protozoa and bacteria that live in their stomachs is passed out in their droppings, which, when mixed with soil, become the material for their mounds and nests.

I've come to Timber Creek because I've heard that Sonia Tidemann, a research scientist for the Conservation Commission of the Northern Territory, and Nancy Burley, an American biologist from the University of Illinois, will be trapping lots of finches. Nancy had hooked up with Sonia by radio telephone when she heard Sonia was getting scores of zebra finches in her mist nets, hundreds at some trap sites. Sonia had been trapping for three weeks. With the help of a volunteer from England, she had managed to band over 2,000 finches: pictorellas, chestnut-breasted finches, long-tailed finches, masked finches, double-barred finches, zebra finches, Gouldian finches.

For several years while working on her Ph.D. dissertation on three species of fairy wrens near Booligal, New South Wales, Sonia collected all kinds of data on breeding patterns, population dynamics, nest site selection, food preferences, types of vegetation, insect abundance. Working along creek edges and swamps and in open flat expanses of shrubland, Sonia sought to answer the tenacious question of how closely related species can coexist without one or more of them being disadvantaged through competition. Her answers proved to be both unsurprising and perplexing. She found that each of the fairy wrens selected different parts of the bush in which to feed and rear offspring, as if avoiding competition, but that when insects were abundant there was so much food around that different species of birds fed on the same critters.

Sonia wondered if there is such a thing as competition. Although there may have been plenty of competition in the past among fairy wrens in western New South Wales, this was not something she could measure. As for the present, she concluded only that each of the three species of fairy wrens has a discrete and yet obviously successful strategy for existing in its semi-arid environment.

Nancy Burley is a different kind of biologist. Nancy is preoccupied with the evolution of mating patterns in birds. For several years she's maintained a colony of more than 500 zebra finches in large indoor aviaries at the University of Illinois, where she tries to understand what males and females find attractive in one another. She's made a number of exciting discoveries, all of them in the laboratory. Now she's come to Outback Australia to see whether the third most popular cage bird in the world, after budgerigars and canaries, behaves more or less like its wild ancestor. If it doesn't, she's in trouble.

Since Nancy began work on the zebra finch in the late 1970s, initially at McGill University in Montreal and then at the University of Illinois in Urbana, she has made a great many ornithologists and biologists stand up and take notice. In a series of long-term breeding experiments, she's been able to mimic the process of evolution through the use of colored leg bands, a kind of pseudo-genetic mutation. Among other things, she's found that zebra finches wearing certain colors (red for males, black for females) are considerably more attractive to members of the opposite sex. These attractive individuals have many more offspring, sometimes engage in bigamous behavior (the finches were supposed to be monogamous), live longer, and spend less time sharing household duties in the nest. Unattractive zebra finches, males with green leg bands and females with blue bands (colors not found on their bodies, unlike red and black), have a hard time finding mates, have to work longer hours when they do become parents, and die at a younger age. Both attractive and unattractive birds seem to kill their young selectively, sparing those whose sex coincides with that of the more attractive parent.

Nancy's discoveries imply that the research findings of more than fifty years of fieldwork on color-banded birds are suspect. If a piece of colored "jewelry" makes a bird more or less attractive and thereby affects social and sexual behavior in non-random ways, then how can one who has used colored leg bands to iden-

tify individual birds be certain that his findings are legitimate?
Furthermore, it has long been thought that monogamous birds
like zebra finches have little potential for evolving new characteristics through heightened sexual attractiveness; if there aren't
significant differences in number of offspring among individuals
(an assumption usually made about monogamous species by
biologists), then there's no way for individuals with distinctive
genes and special attributes to gain a selective advantage.

A further implication of Nancy's work is that zebra finches
are amazingly plastic and adaptable in what they're capable of
doing, given the right circumstances. As obnoxious as the idea
may be to humans, it may be "right" in an evolutionary sense
for an animal to engage in infanticide if this increases the
number of surviving descendants of a parent that nurtures sons
but kills daughters (or vice versa). Zebra finches make these
hard, calculating "decisions" with skill and accuracy. Birds, one
might legitimately conclude from Nancy's pioneering work, are
hardly the possessors of bird brains. In fact, they're capable of
complex and sophisticated decisions about the only thing that
in the long-run matters: the production of healthy offspring that
will reproduce.

The first morning out, down the road a couple of dozen
kilometers from Timber Creek, Sonia turns her four-wheel-
drive Toyota off the narrow bitumen road and charges ahead
onto a seldom-used station road. Then, seemingly in the middle
of nowhere, driving via some vague map in her head, Sonia turns
left and we're weaving cross-country among second growth
trees, thinning patches of black spear grass.

"This is it, the site," Sonia exclaims. "The creek's just over
there." She points.

All I see are twisted thorny shrubs, a dead tree trunk chewed
to bits by tropical insects, bleached grass, smooth-skinned boab
trees, arching acacias and eucalpyts.

We get out of the truck and tramp through reedy grass up to
our chests. Sonia's barefoot.

"There are death adders and king browns here, aren't there?"
I say.

Sonia nods. "Especially around water."

I see a black pool ahead of us, a billabong. I recall reading a few days earlier about an Aussie who stayed in a motel in Larrimah. He picked up a king brown in the garden patio, got bit, spent five days in the hospital, and nearly died. He was young, well over 200 pounds. I look down at my low-cut Nikes, over at Nancy's equally inadequate Reeboks. At least we're wearing long pants. Sonia is wearing shorts.

Since Sonia has never mist-netted this particular billabong before, it's a bit of a guessing game as to where to put the nets. So we put up two of them along one elongated muddy edge, another angled at one of the rocky corners, a fourth on the other side. Then it's time to go back to the Land Cruiser, take out a folding table, chairs and a tackle box full of small tools and bird banding gear, and set them up, to collect the same sorts of data again and again until you begin to think that science is more boring than working on a six-motion assembly line.

With Nancy and Sonia, science goes something like this. Band the birds with uniquely numbered aluminum rings. Weigh the birds and estimate how much food is in their crops. (Crops are rather transparent expandable pouches on either side of a bird's neck that, when full, bring to mind giant tumors.) If the seeds in the crop look abundant enough and varied enough in size and color, stick a plastic tube deep into the bird's throat and pull some out for laboratory analysis. Draw a bit of blood from under a wing, then blow the blood through a slender piece of glass called a capillary tube onto a glass slide. Smear the blood with another slide; do it just right, so that the blood cells are spread as evenly as possible. Later you'll be able to find out whether the birds harbor parasites. Now measure tail length and distance from the back of the head to the tip of the bill. Do these things because . . . well, at least partly because it's a tradition among ornithologists to do so. You never know; the information might come in handy. After the measurements are taken, hand the pliant ruffled little creature over to Nancy. She spreads a wing, sticks her nose into the feathers and, in arcane numerical code, describes to Sonia how much it's molting on its body, its tail, its wing feathers. Then—deliciously let it be said—she digs into her two-volume set of Munsell color chips to match them against bill color and eye color and leg color with more precision on hue and chroma than would be imagined by a paintmaker.

But before all this can get underway, there has to be something in the nets, the right kind of something—finches only, please! Rufous-throated honeyeaters, plump diamond doves, walkabout spinifex pigeons, mean-beaked butcherbirds, dainty red-backed fairy wrens, howling blue-winged kookaburras, cackling crows count for almost nothing. They're just extra work, birds to be taken out of the nets as carefully and quickly as possible, perhaps held for a long moment and just admired, or contemplated for future reference and some abstract theory about ecology or social behavior that runs loose in the head.

So you wait: twenty minutes, a half-hour. You wonder if by chance you're at one of those watering holes that Aborigines brought to the attention of early explorers, places where zebra finches, then called waxbills or chestnut-eared finches, were said to flock by the tens of thousands. It was alleged that they could be measured by the acre, in numbers so large that zebra finches became the Aboriginal standard of numerical vastness in a land as vast as any on the face of the earth. If you asked an Aboriginal man if there were lots of kangaroos in his country, he might give you one of two stories. If he didn't want to be bothered, he'd say, "They done finish altogether long time." But if he thought that you wanted meat and would share some of your take with him and he knew where they were abundant, he'd say, "The 'roos sit down like a mob of waxbills." Aborigines also greatly valued the excrement of the tiny zebra finch. They made it into a paste that was rubbed on the temples and forehead to cure all manner of illness.

In the famous four-volume 1894 *Report on the Work of the Horn Scientific Expedition to Central Australia*, it was noted:

> The approach to a water-hole can always be told, not only
> by the greener patches of scrub and trees immediately sur-
> rounding the water, but by the twittering of innumerable
> chestnut-eared finches. The twittering of these pretty little
> birds may always be taken as an indication that water is not

far away: from the side of a water-hole flocks rise as you approach, and their little grass nests are very common. . . . They fall an easy prey to such birds as the falcons, which will swoop down upon a flock and usually carry off a little finch each time. Judging by their numbers they must be prolific breeders.

After World War II cattlemen put down bores and sunk numerous wells, thereby greatly extending the availability of water for livestock, feral animals, kangaroos. Perhaps the additional water increased the numbers and range of finches for a very short time after a bore was sunk or a well dug. Trees remained and nesting sites were available, and at least for a couple of years there was probably more diversity in the plant life around a bore or well. Then, as the plant life came under constant attack by kangaroos and large four-footed animals—cattle, feral horses, feral donkeys—and began to simplify and disappear, even the trees were destroyed through too much browsing.

Maybe there are now many fewer zebra finches in any given year in the Centre than there were prior to the sinking of all these bores. Maybe when there are good rains and lots of grasses, the finches congregate around water and this gives a false impression of vast numbers. Can the numbers be greater if hundreds of thousands of square kilometers of rich annual grasses in the Centre have been lost, if there's been much greater demand placed on all grasses, if there are fewer desirable nesting sites because tens of thousands of trees around bores have been killed or made useless by too much browsing?

Is it now possible for anyone to know the answers to the questions that are of particular interest to biologists like Sonia Tidemann and Nancy Burley?

"Let's check the nets," Sonia says.

Nancy's ready, I'm not. Nancy's had experience with mist netting, and more than just a little with handling finches; 50,000 times or so might be a reasonable estimate. But for me, it's all pretty much a mystery. What, in particular, do I do when I come upon a bird so tangled in black nylon that it makes a fisherman's knotted line look like a first grade arithmetic problem? Can I be careful enough to avoid breaking a leg or a wing or a neck of a bird that doesn't weigh much more than a good slice of lemon?

I don't kill or maim a bird, but then I'm so slow I might just as well be put out to pasture. Nancy and Sonia whip back and forth around me with three and four birds per hand, hurrying to deftly untangle one more victim before putting it in a white calico bag. How do they do it, I wonder, nothing but pure envy in my heart? And how can they possibly hold that many birds in hand without letting them go or squeezing them to death?

As it turns out, it's all pretty simple. Follow these rules. First, find out which way the bird flew into the net; screw up here and it's almost certain you'll want to scream from frustration. Then you're off and running. Take each leg and gently pull and pull until the long-clawed toes and the leg are free. Next, find the fine mesh caught between the body and the wings and pull it over the wing shoulder and away from the bird. Lastly, just keep looping the black nylon mesh over the bird's head—to the left or to the right—until it's free. Then the bird is free to fly, and break away from a fumbling hand it will if you're a green-eared novice. Then you learn the trick of sticking the bird's neck between your first and second fingers and holding your fingertips together.

"You ever killed one this way?" I ask Nancy.

"Other ways, yes. Holding them like that, never."

"Never?"

"Never," she insists. "It's much easier to squeeze the life out of them by holding them around the breast."

We work all day. We catch hundreds of birds, nearly two hundred finches, several different species. Throughout the day we'd heard dozens of zebra finches singing, but we catch not a single one in the nets. Sonia doesn't know why. Nancy doesn't know why. Now there is another unanswered question in a growing list.

Flies, flies, flies! Do bushflies have no other purpose in life than to swarm the faces of sweating humans? Lazy sorts who like to sleep in, the dastardly buzzers make up for their indolent ways as soon as they get the scent of warm wet meat. They work us over all day long. Oh, how they love the human face! The ears, the cheeks, the ticklish corners of lips, eyelids and eyelashes and eyebrows, just those spots on the edges of my beard where a tickle demands a slap. They swoop, they circle, they alight, their numbers multiply. They're fearless.

In his memoirs, Archer Russell, a self-described "tramp-royal" who spent the better part of 1928 and 1929 exploring the Centre, wrote:

> We built smoke smudges to drive them away, we stood in the smoke of the fires until water fell from our eyes, we ate our food standing over the fires—it was all of no avail. The flies ate us and we ate the flies—literally and in quantity. They bit us and they stung us, they crawled up our nostrils and buzzed in our ears. Life . . . becomes a torture. The human is driven to the point of desperation, the stock and the wild animals of the bush to the verge of madness. Bitten and stung, the eyes of the stock go red and raw, and deep holes the size of a shilling piece are eaten into the corners; horses and the wild animals of the bush go blind. Bung-eyes, fly-sickness accompanied by severe vomiting, dysentery in its worst form, and Barcoo Rot, causing chronic sores on the hands and face, become the lot of the human.

No explorer into central Australia failed to mention bush flies frequently in his journal. They were described as swarming in colossal clouds, as being so numerous as to turn camels black, as eating holes as large as a U.S. fifty-cent piece below the eyes of horses, as being particularly troublesome in cattle country, in warm weather after a rain. Explorers felt a perverse sense of joy when they came upon large patches of sundew plants and saw the leaves thickly covered with flies glued to the plants' sticky secretions. They were relieved at sundown when the flies went off to roost on the tips of leaves and twigs, even though this meant that it was now time for mosquitoes to take over, or ants, if you were bedding down under or too near an ironwood tree or on a claypan.

White explorers invariably were envious of Aborigines. They

couldn't understand how these natives could simply lie down in a swarm of flies and fall asleep with perhaps nothing more than a skimpy hat covering their faces. Many Outback cowboys have not been too macho to wear fly veils that fit around the crowns of their hats and hang down to their shoulders. The veils, made of quarter-inch mesh, allow the flies in, but the movement of the veil makes them quickly depart.

Gray, with clear wings and a black first segment of the abdomen, the common bushfly is native to Australia. With the exception of forests, it's found just about everywhere on the continent. It's no more than half the bulk of a common housefly, but it's much more tenacious. It often doesn't heed what's jokingly known as the Australian salute, the swishing hand in front of the face; and after a while one senses that the persistent little critters laugh at those little old ladies from Perth and Peoria who strut around wearing hats with corks dangling from brim line to chin.

The bushfly is susceptible to extremes of temperature and is virtually nonexistent in cold winters in the Centre. During a mild winter, like this one, some will survive and multiply. Their numbers will shoot skyward if there's been some winter rain to bring on nectar-full blossoms, their source of sugar and water. Rain also affects pasture growth, which in turn affects the dung in which they breed and multiply. Moist dung allows maggots to thrive.

The smell of fresh dung is irresistible to flies. Their eggs are deposited exclusively in dung; the dung of horses, cattle, emu, kangaroos, man—just about any kind of excrement will do. Bushflies can live for nine weeks or more, and the female may lay as many as 250 eggs at a half-dozen different sites. Though willy-wagtails and a few other birds are adept enough to make a meal of bushflies, they have no widespread voracious predators to keep their numbers down.

When bushflies come upon humans they look for a place out of the wind, or for those choice spots that have ample moisture: the eyes, the nose, the mouth, wounds. Bushflies do not actually bite, but they do have prestomal "teeth" on the proboscis that allow them to open old wounds and rasp away at soft tissue. When they eat—actually, food can be taken only in liquid form by the proboscis—they eat selectively: blood and pus, milk and tears, they're all good sources of protein. They even like sweat and urine. Without water bushflies can survive only about fifteen hours on a summer day. Without some form of energy they die within two days. Without protein female flies cannot develop their eggs and complete their life cycle, which is the reason that most bushflies that settle on humans are females.

"Oh, sugah!" Sonia says. "He got him." She screws up her mouth while drawing our attention to a spot not twenty-five feet from where we sit, beneath the shade of an old cabbage gum. I jerk my head around and see the sleek brown falcon, the bulk of his well-defined body stretched a good foot or more above the parched sock-high grass and weeds, proud as a tyrannical king at court, daring us to approach.

One of Australia's most widespread and abundant raptors, the brown falcon has distinctive double-moustache markings and a pale cheek patch, a hooked grey bill that acts as meat hook and pliers and fork, sooty-brown and buff wing feathers that spread to three feet in flight. It rarely hunts for prey on the wing, preferring to search by sitting quietly on a high perch. A real gourmand, the brown falcon loves variety: lizards, snakes, young rabbits, mice, caterpillars, grasshoppers, crickets, beetles, small birds. What a marvelous invention of nature these raptors are, I think one moment, and then otherwise when I hear the ring of Sonia's words.

"Damn! A long-tailed finch we just banded."

I strain to see the victim. I look for some telltale sign that Sonia's wrong. But the talons are too big, the finch too small, the grass too high. Then I see that she's right.

In the name of science we'd kept the little guy in a bag, without food. We'd taken blood from a vein beneath a wing, made him weak.

We'd seen the falcon earlier that morning atop the very highest branch of a burned Darwin box tree, not far from the murky green water hole where we'd put up three mist nets. Each of the nets was forty feet in length, about six feet high, made of three-quarter-inch black nylon mesh. We'd pushed the supporting wooden poles into packed dirt and secured them with rope and tent stakes, then carefully stretched the nets to create ample pockets for finches to drop into after hitting the nets on their way to or from water. The whole time we worked in the soft early morning light the falcon hardly moved from his lofty perch. He watched us with the attentiveness of a bank robber planning a heist, fully aware of his source of meals in the nearby trees, old gums and ironwoods often chockablock with fairy wrens, honeyeaters, thornbills, birds whose names I'd never heard before coming to Australia.

Mere seconds after we'd left the water hole and walked through black spear grass and kangaroo grass to return to the Toyota Land Cruiser and set up camp, the falcon zoomed in on a rufous-throated honeyeater. He somehow missed the easy kill. Then Sonia shouted and gave chase. But the day, as the falcon knew better than we, had just begun.

We've still not caught any zebra finches; they're on Nancy's mind. I lament the loss of the long-tailed finch. Nancy tells me about the constant fight of all small birds to escape the clutches of larger predators. She mentions predation rates on zebra finches near Alice Springs that make death from lung cancer sound like a rare event. Aware that they're a favored meal for birds like crows and butcherbirds, the finches build their nests well within the prickly tight tangle of corkwood needles or prickly wattle, or within the gut of another nettlesome bush inhospitable to large birds, dead finish. It's a bold, incautious and stupid butcherbird or crow that will fly headlong through a gauntlet of spears in search of finches in their nests. Finches, it seems, often choose older corkwoods in which to begin a new generation. In these older trees the bores of limbs are festooned with fisty accumulations of dead needles, "decoy" nests that make a predator's search for the real ones time-consuming.

But zebra finches don't always win their battle to avoid the butcherbird and the mean-looking hook at the end of its threatening gray beak. Nancy tells a story of a pied butcherbird catching a zebra finch at one of her traps in Alice Springs. After the butcherbird killed the finch it took it over to an ironwood tree and wedged its head into the fork of a branch. Then it meticulously pulled out the finch's tail feathers, poked a hole in the corpse and slurped up its innards. After eating more of the lower half of the finch, the butcherbird bit the upper half in two, gave the breast to one of its dependent young and the head and the beak to another one. The butcherbird had done such a masterly job of inserting the finch in the branch that the whole time it worked over the finch it did so without the use of its feet.

Still no zebra finches in the nets. But then, no Gouldian finches either. Why not?

Nancy is frustrated, puzzled, quiet. Sonia, however, likes to ruminate out loud about the fate of the Gouldian finch, that adorable little gem with a purple breast, a yellow belly, and a black or red head that brings to mind an understated nun's hood. Once widespread throughout the grassy subcoastal woodlands of northern Australia, the Gouldian finch is now absent from at least half of its former range. In Western Australia, where fifty years ago there were tens of thousands of Gouldians, there are now hundreds. Travelers in the 1930s remarked that "the trees were white with screeching corellas and small cockatoos. Vast numbers of Gouldian and other finches were taken at isolated water holes."

Has intense trapping, long illegal in the Northern Territory, been largely responsible for the demise of the Gouldian? Or have they been victimized by insensitive range practices of cattle station owners, widespread destruction of native perennial grasses through too frequent burning of the rank understory to create sweet green for cattle?

In this part of the Outback, known as The Top End, about half of the forests and woodlands are burned each year, and most are burned again within a span of two to three years. Typically, pastoralists begin burning in the middle of what is known as The Dry. They continue burning until the heavy rains of The Wet, which begin between October and December. In recent years there has been heightened awareness among conservationists and scientists that while purposeful burning itself is not bad, timing can be critical. Waiting until well into The Dry to start fires insures that grasses and trees will burn more fiercely and completely. Hot midseason fires destroy the flowers of trees and diminish fruit production later in the year. Because of the nature of contemporary burning practices, open forests in The Top End have suffered massive reductions in fruit-producing species. It's safe to assume that this has greatly affected the abundance and diversity of fruit-eating animals.

Much could have been learned, and still can be, from ancient Aboriginal practices. Aborigines tended to burn early in The Dry, with the result that fires were patchy, often covered small areas, and did not so thoroughly scorch trees. They used fire, or "munwag," to manage the resources of their environment. They recognized that different kinds of vegetation have their own ignition and fire persistence characteristics. When they burned open forests they were careful to protect fruit-bearing trees. In some areas they didn't burn at all; in others—around water—they never failed to burn in order to produce feed to draw in animals.

One significant result of distinguishing among different vegetational habits and of burning selectively and early was the creation of a vegetational mosaic. With patchy burning and with fires set at different times of the year, animals and plants had more refuges in which to survive and reproduce. In making judicious use of what has been called "fire stick farming," Aborigines insured themselves of seasonal and yearly harvests of plants and animals.

Aborigines used fires for many other reasons: to clear trails, to signal, to flush out reptiles and small mammals from the undergrowth, to increase their visibility in forest or tall grass, to clear areas of litter so that they could more easily dig up food plants or search for insect larvae, to fell dead trees for firewood. It may even be that since their arrival in Australia more than 40,000 years ago, Aborigines have, through burning, caused the extinction of numerous native plants and animals. Be this as it may, it would seem that their methods were less destructive and did more to ensure the persistence of most species of plants and animals than do those currently employed.

We drive 240 kilometers before dawn to get to a "turkey nest," a water reservoir made by moving earth with a tractor and blade to form a huge reserve tank for cattle. As we set up the mist nets at the top of the turkey nest Sonia expresses confidence that we'll finally catch zebra finches. Before we've put up the third net we catch a couple of long-tailed finches in the first one. We've been catching the long-tails by the bushel. Nancy has become fascinated with their needle-like black tails, which are almost as long as the rest of their bodies.

She'd love to take a ruler and scissors to their tails, perhaps even glue extra feathers to some tails to make them as long as pencils, and then do everything possible to get them to breed as wildly as their natural ways will allow. The question would be this: With shorter tails, will the long-tailed finches be less attractive to one another? Would they appear to be less healthy, to have inferior genes, be forced to take whomever's left over, not have what it takes to produce large broods of sexy sons and daughters? With extra long tails, will males have their pick of females? And will they—faithful sorts that they're supposed to be—become sneaky philanderers if that most unusual phallic ornament proves utterly irresistible to female eyes?

What we see this bright and cloudless morning far from a madding crowd is portentous, depressing, exhilarating. The lip of the turkey nest is surrounded by tall grass and swamp reeds, scraggly second-growth acacia, and, down on the level, more thick grass and lots of prickly turpentine trees that are unkind to man and beast alike. There's a crack in the turkey nest; with all this water and moisture and high grass around, the site is ideal for the aggressive king brown snake. I'm dying to see my first one, to see whether it looks as mean as it ought to with all that deadly poison in its bite. Sonia, I gather, would rather not. For the first time, she's decided that it's prudent to put on a pair of leather boots.

Except for a small line of sparsely vegetated mountains to the southwest and trickling lines of Brahmas and shorthorns on the slow march to water, the long view from atop the turkey nest brings to mind a single word: abuse. Beneath the beaten and

shriveled acacias I see little but hard rock, soil raped and trampled far too many times, only the slightest hint of life. It's true,
we're in the middle of what station owners call the sacrifice
area, those several kilometers of land around water where nothing palatable has a chance to reach its teenage years.

This cattle station is owned by Indonesians. At dinner the
night before, the station manager claimed that he was running
25,000 head of cattle, an incredible number for a station of fewer
than 3,000 square kilometers.

Sonia, looking for baseline information on finches, especially
Gouldians, asked him, "What is your concept of conservation?"

"We clear a few weeds when they get in the way. We poison
dingoes. We shoot donkeys and horses."

This far western section of the Northern Territory, described
by early explorers as "splendidly grassed," is now pauperized. It
has few trees, few grasses, few bushes—in many places, none at
all. It's pretty certain that all kinds of native wildlife, resident
on this land for thousands of years, are gone forever from this
and similar cattle stations. Among the list of victims are buff-
sided robins, purple-crowned wrens, burrowing bettongs, red-
tailed phascagoles, golden bandicoots, golden-backed tree rats.

Massive, irreversible changes came about because of greed,
colossal and continuous overstocking of cattle that began in the
nineteenth century. It was a long time before fences were built,
and, owing to scarce water, cattle were herded in untold numbers along river frontages and alluvial flats. With no plant cover
left, torrential downpours gullied and eroded. Rain has washed
away tens of millions of tons of soil that had taken thousands of
years to make.

We catch a score of long-tailed and masked finches in the nets.
We free them, bag them by species, and return to camp, where
we set them in the shade beneath the Land Rover. Sonia and
Nancy immediately start taking the birds through the gauntlet
of scientific analyses. For a while I act as scribe to quicken the
pace. Then, my fascination with the whole affair really centered
on trapping and freeing birds, I take a break to check the nets.

I find that except for a couple of careless honeyeaters, not so easily freed, the nets are empty. Is the problem the sneaky brown goshawk that flew in and began scaring off birds just about the time we arrived? We couldn't be sure from our sighting, but maybe it was a female goshawk that we'd seen, one who'd told her mate to quit being an inconsiderate chauvinist and sit on the eggs for an hour or two while she went looking for food. Unable to see anything resembling a small head with a curved black beak above brown and creamy striped plumage in the greenery of the mature trees, I return to camp thinking, Why worry? It's still early, the goshawk's sure to get impatient and try another site; we're netting the only water in the dry creek . . . or are we? Is there water nearby that we're unaware of and need to cover up?

Sonia and I walk and hop among the angular flat black rocks of the creek, upstream for half a mile or so. So far the morning is pleasantly cool, breezeless, free of buzzing insects; it fits no image I have of this part of the tropics at this time of year. We talk about Sonia's impressions on moving to Darwin: liking it more than she had imagined coming from the south; loving her work and staying out bush for weeks at a time; being shocked by the price of housing; delighted by her daughter's happiness with the boarding school in which she's enrolled.

Sonia and I see not the slightest trickle of water, so we backtrack. Soon Nancy joins us. We sit on large rocks in the middle of the river bed, enjoy the chattering and singing around us, each others' company. Sonia identifies wild plum trees, others that border the creek. Now and again we pick up binoculars and look at the mist nets to see whether the finches are cooperating.

Suddenly, Sonia and Nancy tune in to the familiar song of double-barred finches in the tangled roots and branches of a wild plum that can't decide whether to commit its future to the bank above or the eroding stony dirt wall below. Nancy goes into a trance.

For several years in her Illinois lab she has maintained a colony of them. Their numbers have grown from twenty to more than forty. She's had the uncommon good luck of successfully breeding them in captivity without having finches of other species raise their young (a common aviary practice in the U.S.)

and thereby bastardizing them for scientific inquiry by imprinting them with alien social habits. All of this was necessary if Nancy was to use the double-barred finch to demonstrate that the spectacular and quite controversial results she got with zebra finches are not confined to a single species. This she has begun to show with the bird she's wont to call an owl finch, a very appropriate name, you'd agree, given its unmistakable owl-like face.

Nancy needs as much varied evidence as possible. As she has come up with more and more startling results and gained a larger audience, fewer professional biologists have been able to ignore her claims that zebra finches discriminate among each other on the basis of slight differences in appearance. "Oh no, what you're telling us can't be true," many have privately and publicly told Nancy in recent years. "It would mean that what I and hundreds of other experts have written about color-banded bird populations might be suspect, even wrong! Zebra finches couldn't possibly be that willing to change their social and sexual behavior merely because they'd been given a piece of plastic jewelry and now see themselves as uncommonly sexy, more nattily dressed for the serious business of courting and mating."

Nancy's an original, but she's not a whole-cloth original. More than a hundred years ago, Charles Darwin suggested that understanding the ways in which birds bring color to their feathers and display themselves to one another would tell us why some are healthy and robust and immensely successful at producing young, while others are reproductively inept and over time most certainly will lose the battle for representation in nature's house of bird genes.

Even before we've finished putting up the last of four mist nets, there are birds of all manner of description seemingly everywhere. Honeyeaters, diamond doves, zebra finches, double-barred finches, masked finches—all of them singing and diving among the lean acacias, zooming into the nets, squabbling with one another for best spot and first drink along a small beach at water's edge.

On the flat at the base of the turkey nest an army of proud fat spinifex pigeons is strutting through soil-poor canyons of small sharp rocks. They roll on, under the barbed wire fence, through mud and grass and weeds, up the hill, out of sight. Only my presence causes them to detour slightly from a well-worn track. Not far from where we've strung a large tarpaulin to protect us from the sun while working over birds are scores of happy zebra finches flitting among the inner branches of gnarled turpentine trees. Now and then they land on a small clearing among bleached grasses; they scour the rippled earth for seeds.

Twenty yards to the east, crowds of galahs and ravens perch in gum trees above two long iron cattle troughs. The galahs are clearing their throats, gossiping like old ladies gone crazy, yelling at the shorthorns and ugly-eared Brahmas to move over so they can get a good drink before getting on with the day's business.

While Sonia and Nancy work at an unnerving pace, I stalk all this memorable birdlife. I get caught up in a tree full of zebra finches, watching them chirp for pleasure, sing for love, hug and snuggle up. I stare, fascinated by the masterly skill with which the males groom their mates, the professional head rubs they administer. I jump back and forth between birds and humans, wondering: Is there a female animal anywhere in the world that doesn't relish a head rub? Maybe even more than sex?

Nancy and Sonia push on, harder. We've only got a couple of days of trapping left before Nancy must return to Alice Springs, Sonia to other assignments. Nancy works furiously now that the nets and the calico bags are full of zebra finches. To a scientist, everything ultimately becomes a matter of statistical significance, sample size, getting enough numbers to test a hypothesis or two. Nancy would like data on about two hundred zebra finches from this part of Australia, enough to be able to say that the bill and plumage colors and sex ratio in this alternating wet-dry northern environment either are or are not like what she's starting to find in the more arid environs of Alice Springs.

Both Sonia and Nancy have a clearly conceived stake in getting seventy-five or a hundred of four different species of finches typed for blood. They've been talking madly about measuring parasite load. What kind of parasites will they find? And how many? Will the number of blood parasites bear any relationship to beak color patterns? Perhaps to weight and feather condition? In Alice Springs, Nancy has already started collecting ectoparasites, tiny creatures such as mites and lice found on the bodies of finches.

After poking a finch's head through a large piece of cloth and grasping it delicately by the neck, its body is more or less sealed inside a tin container with chloroform. The chloroform anaesthetizes the mites and lice, which then drop onto a piece of white paper. The paper is put under a microscope to identify the animals that feed on the finch's feathers and body.

For a number of years now, Nancy and her students in Illinois have spent hundreds of hours recording the color of finch legs and beaks. She's had more than an iffy hunch that the color of the beak varies in predictable ways between the sexes, and according to where the birds are in their reproductive cycle. The beaks generally are redder in the male, more orange in the female. The colors get paler when the birds are in poor health, toward the end of a breeding cycle when they've expended a good deal of energy to raise the young. But what else do changes in color represent? Are darker and brighter colors in the male indicative of greater attractiveness? Or greater aggressiveness? Or better health? Do the females recognize and heed these differences when choosing a life-long mate? What is Nancy to make of her lab finding that female beak colors show much greater variation than those of males? What is it about the evolution of male zebra finches that has made them more conservative in beak color variation? Will the same patterns that she's found in an artificial environment in Illinois also show up in nature?

Is there any correlation between beak coloration patterns and either blood parasites or ectoparasites? The idea Nancy wants to test is simple enough. Since parasites have such short generation times and, in theory, can have such devastating effects on the health of birds, they just might play a major role in a bird's mating and reproductive history. Just might, for at this stage the whole idea is a hypothesis dreamed up in an air-conditioned office at the University of Michigan several years ago. If this hypothesis has any real substance to it, less healthy birds—those with greater parasite loads—will have paler beaks. They'll be less attractive, get second-class mates, produce fewer offspring, inferior offspring, perhaps even die at a younger age.

It's late afternoon. We're tired and cranky. We're trying to do our best by the finches. Since they've been in a calico bag for up to four hours without food or drink and then have had to suffer the loss of blood, Sonia and Nancy hold them and gaze at them with motherly concern. They give them a good drink of water before putting them in a small wooden cage. There they can quiet down, have all the food and water they desire, regain lost strength. But we can't keep them overnight. We'll be leaving at sundown. The birds will have to be given time to return to their homes, find their mates, perhaps forage for more food to regurgitate later to the young they're now raising.

The falcon's nowhere in sight, so a half-dozen masked and long-tailed finches are simultaneously released from the small holding cage. They fly up, down, and away at acute angles. They sing; they seem to be bursting with joy to be free.

Catching us in a relaxed moment, the falcon rushes in and scores. He deftly hits a masked finch who took off too slowly, too close to the ground, on too predictable a trajectory.

I see a talon tightly gripping the dying victim. I stare at the falcon; he stares back at me. Before I'm able to attribute motive to action and make human what is subject to a somewhat different set of laws, he takes off, rises to mid-tree level, and cruises onto a flat knoll sixty yards away.

I pick up binoculars and immediately bring him into focus. He's already at work. Feathers are floating upward, his deadly beak is ripping at the warm body. As if to remind us whose territory we've barged into, he tears off the tiny head of the masked finch and crunches down on its daisy-yellow beak.

The falcon finishes his meal. He flaps his wings and lazily flies off. I follow him with the glasses until I lose sight of him. I remind myself that I too love to eat flesh.

A SIDELONG
LOOK AT ALICE

On Todd Street, Alice Springs' main drag, I stroll past old gray tourists in sneakers and sun hats, young scruffy sorts with backpacks and the look of too much sun, several circular clusters of Aborigines on lawns. The Aboriginal women are spindly-legged, barefoot. Their hair, their dresses, their blouses are messy and dirty. They're drinking Coca-Cola, eating out of Kentucky Fried Chicken boxes, breast-feeding children just as they would out in the bush. The Aboriginal men are wearing cowboy boots and hats, visored caps advertising PEUGEOT and CAT.

Inside the modern one-story brick town council building with the long sloping tile roof, a cheerful redheaded woman gives me several brochures. She seems pleased to answer questions. I discover that Alice Springs has somewhere in the neighborhood of 25,000 people, and that during the high tourist season, May to August, the population is almost half again as large. More than 200,000 tourists a year come to The Alice, about ten times the number that came two decades ago. Three-quarters of them visit Uluru (Ayers Rock) and nearby Mount Olga. The Alice has a casino, eight travel agencies, a handful of rent-a-car outlets, a score of tour operators, more than fifteen gift and souvenir shops, a dozen caravan parks, twenty-five hotels and motels with more than a thousand rooms, and an exorbitantly priced, 252-room Sheraton that serves barbecued kangaroo T-bone with witchetty grub sauce. Witchetty grubs are a favorite Aboriginal food, and steaks covered with a sauce prepared from the grubs are the number one choice among tourists who frequent the town's most popular restaurant.

Inside the town council building is a large scale model of what Alice Springs is supposed to look like in another two decades. The model is mind-boggling, unsettling. I see absolutely nothing in The Alice of the future that bears any resemblance to its Aboriginal past, to the splendor or mysteries of the deserts that stretch for more than a thousand miles in every direction around the town, to its unique and special history of pioneer settlement, its vast cattle stations. The town of the future, it seems, could easily have been conceived by a dreamy young architect who had never ventured beyond Sydney or Melbourne.

There are numerous reminders that Alice Springs is an isolated town, a long, long way from coastal, urban Australia. There's a single television station. There's one drive-in theater open three nights a week, and an arts center that sometimes screens movies on weekends. The Alice has never had a "real" movie theater. For decades it did have two little walk-in square boxes in the center of town, but both of them were roofless. One was multi-purpose and used only by whites. When a movie wasn't showing, the folding chairs were pushed against the walls and the floor was used for skating or dancing. The other theater operated only on Friday nights. It screened mainly westerns and was meant to serve the Aboriginal population. For many Aborigines, it was their first opportunity to learn the difference between fact and fiction.

Dick Kimber, a longtime resident of Alice Springs, tells of the time when the western film star, Audie Murphy, was being attacked by desperadoes. While he fended them off with a volley of gunshots, an Indian slyly approached him from behind. Just as the Indian was about to apply his tomahawk to the back of Audie Murphy's neck, an Aborigine in the front row of the theater stood up and threw an empty bottle at the Indian. The Indian disappeared through the hole in the screen. Several Aborigines, whose proper place was the front three rows, jumped to their feet to cheer.

Like other Outback towns, The Alice has solved its problem of marginal access to television and the products of Hollywood

by turning with a vengeance to video cassettes. Today the town
has no fewer than ten video rental stores. One is so busy it's like
a supermarket, open twelve hours a day every day of the week.
It carries thousands of titles, which, when added to its vast store
of multiple copies, makes it among the largest video rental outlets in the entire country.

I catch the gritty informality as I pass the bouncer at the door
and squeeze among tattered tank tops to a circle of scruffy sorts
sitting on bar stools, the lot of them quaffing beer, grabbing at a
plate of greasy sausages. I step around them, then to one side to
avoid getting scratched by wire cutters sticking out of a back
pocket. I'm momentarily halted by a dusty, tattooed arm tossing
a crushed beer can toward the garbage gutter along a wall. Clang!
The can hits the steel floor railing, bounces into other cans,
potato chip bags, cigarette butts.

On the adjoining wall, behind the pub's pool table, my eyes
land on a mural-sized color photograph of The Bares, the twenty-
five-odd member rugby team that the pub sponsors. Three rows
deep, every last player is nude, one hand barely covering his
evidence of maleness. In the middle of the front row, where I'd
expect to see the captain, a young woman is down on one knee.
She's smiling, she's wearing the team jersey. That's all she's
wearing.

As I get my mug of Castlemaine XXXX, I see a black bouncer
and a short muscular guy in a blue golf shirt trying to drag someone through the pub and out the constricting front door. The
troublemaker is no lightweight; he's giving the two of them a
real go. One bouncer's got him in a head hold. The troublemaker's kicking and flailing away.

There are three bouncers on duty most days after five-thirty,
four on Thursday nights, five on Friday nights. You see them
hanging around the front door, picking up empty glasses, walking to and fro in the unmistakable uniform: neat black slacks, a
pressed white shortsleeve shirt, shined shoes. Some of the bouncers look as if they're on steroids, just in from the iron-pumping
beaches of Queensland's Gold Coast.

They finally get him outside. They tell him to get lost. He throws them a challenging look, curls a hand into a fist. "Go fuck yourself!"

Behind the troublemaker is a slim woman with high cheek-bones and thin lips, fine skin. She's wearing jewelry, a cream cotton dress, white pumps. She looks as if she'd be more at home at The Sheraton Alice, paying one-fifty a night for a room, standing at The Bistro Bar talking smart about the America's Cup.

She scowls, points a defiant finger at the bouncers. She yells, "You bloody no-good nigger. Why don't you get out of here? We don't need you and we don't want you. You have no right to be doing this to him. We'll take you two to court."

Out of nowhere comes a lean sallow-skinned sort, a motorcy-cle helmet in his right hand. He comes to the side of the woman and the troublemaker, and then he throws his head into the black bouncer, then into the white one in the blue golf shirt. "Go fuck your mother!" he screams at both of them. And then again, louder, to make sure he was heard.

The bouncers say nothing.

Someone else decides that they don't like the putdown. A fist flies through the gathering mob and the lightweight defender of the troublemaker is hit square in the jaw. He drops to the sidewalk with a dull thud. His helmet rolls into an earthen de-pression. His mouth opens, a fly circles for a look-see. His hands are open, legs spread. He's motionless, stone-cold out.

No one bothers to worry about the downed intruder for sev-eral long moments. Then the bouncer in the blue golf shirt goes over and tries to give him a hand, slaps him in the face to revive him, helps him to his feet, tells him to get lost before there's more trouble.

"Piss off," the bouncer says. "Don't be a bloody asshole."

The original troublemaker decides to get in a few more blows. He kicks and swings at the golf shirt, at anyone standing nearby. Obviously drunk, he's pushed aside, ignored. So he picks up the closest thing to a weapon he can find: the motorcycle helmet that fell to the ground in the first seconds of round one for the lightweight. He swings the helmet high and twice slams the golf shirt directly on top of the head. The golf shirt drops to his knees, but somehow he doesn't fall on his face. Four bruisers rush in, grab the troublemaker by the hair, the ears, the neck. They gouge his eyes. They slug him in the face, the neck, the midsection. His lips flush, begin to resemble an overripe tomato.

But the troublemaker is as pliant as a punching bag, and he's a hard one to convince that he's outnumbered. He stands, staggers, sways, revives, continues to mouth familiar expletives. His blond female companion looks befuddled, perhaps suddenly eager for the genteel corridors of The Sheraton Alice.

And then it's retribution time. The husky golf shirt with the watermelon arms gets to his feet, picks up the motorcycle helmet, and approaches the troublemaker. Like a discus thrower he brings the helmet behind him and low to the ground, then swings it with all his might. He slams the troublemaker square on the side of the head. It's a crunching, booming, scary knockout: iron knuckles times two. The troublemaker hits the pavement on a dead freefall, another one stone-cold out.

My ears fill with the rousing shouting around me, people taking sides. I wonder if the twenty or so tough guys standing outside this Outback animal house are going to start a free-for-all. A fist to the closest chin, a foot to the groin.

Finally they revive the stupid drunken victim. His female friend now has no time for dirty words, threatened lawsuits. She tells someone to call the police, then sticks one, then two, then five fingers in front of her friend's face. She asks him to count. "Are you going to be okay?" she asks.

He stands, staggers, stoops like a crooked stick.

The Northern Territory Police arrive. They're wearing pressed tan trousers, matching short-sleeve shirts, small Gestapo caps with hard visors. They don't have guns, just lots of notebooks and pencils.

The crowd breaks up, heads for the cool air of the pub and another round of green or blue cans. The mood is somber, undecipherable. As I turn to go inside, a skinny barefoot kid, his skin more blue than brown from all the tattoos, derisively calls to the collective gathering of six policemen: "The bloody sunshine boys!"

It's another day in which I find myself furtively glancing at Aboriginal women in public places. Something about their mannerisms and apparent obliviousness to their surroundings makes me think of them as tough and resilient, supremely knowledgeable about how to nurture their young in an ungenerous environment. What communal bonds and oral myths tie them together in the face of the inevitable forces of assimilation?

Many of the Aboriginal men I see on the streets and in the parks, sitting on railroad tracks, or slouched in the shade of Alice's public toilets, leave different impressions. Maybe it has something to do with their camp dogs, which seem as numerous as the men themselves. Maybe it's the squarish, inscrutable faces, the unkempt dusty appearance, so many of them not working. Maybe it's the grog that I see them buying every time I go to the grocery store—the only thing I see so many of them buying.

My thoughts about grog hardened last Saturday morning when I walked past a grocery store a few minutes before nine. In front of the store, across the road on the littered dirt, all along a pine-dressed cyclone fence, I saw squatting, standing, sitting Aboriginal men. Most of them looked bone tired, anticipatory. There wasn't a woman or a child among them. What's going on here? By nine fifteen I'd gotten my answer. The grocery store opened, the cash register began clanging.

Presently the men strolled past me, toward their town camps, into the Todd River, to happy places known only to them. All but a few were carrying a white plastic bag, an easily recognizable gallon or two of the boxed Coolabah wine in each one.

The grocery store where all this happened is a good two miles from the center of The Alice. It stands pretty much alone, no other businesses to help its business. Its offerings are meager and high-priced. But the store, the most accessible to several of the town camps and to the freehold Aboriginal lands of Amoonguna and Santa Teresa, has the distinction of selling more grog than any other outlet in the whole of the Northern Territory.

At least the men are only doing themselves in with alcohol, not petrol. Petrol sniffing is a problem among many Aboriginal boys in central Australia. It causes lead poisoning, kidney and liver damage, psychological problems, death from heart disease. Children aged five to fifteen can be seen walking around with small tin cans bobbing off their chests, secured around the neck with a piece of string. Some of the children keep the cans just below their noses all day long. They say it makes them feel good, happy, able to cope with problems at home.

For the third day in a row I'm walking the zigzagging dry bed of the Todd River. Here and there I come upon small groups of Aboriginal men sitting on a sandy rise in the middle of the river; or forming a circle near the rooty clutches of a river red gum; or backed up against a crumbling bank with their legs half buried in creamy sand. Wherever I see them, they're drinking from bottles and cans.

Downriver, no one in sight, I'm suddenly aware of all the broken glass, the unmistakable preference for certain beers: Victoria Bitter, Foster's Lager. Soon I'm counting crushed green boxes, each of which once contained more than a gallon of Orlando Coolabah Moselle, the cheapest long-drink drunk in the Centre.

I don't go into town camps or walk the Todd River on a day after Aborigines receive their welfare payments from the government. But I hear that at such times small groups explode to drunken gatherings of ten and fifteen, and that there have been times in the recent past when more than 150 Aborigines could be found in the river drinking away their food and clothing, their lives.

The Aborigine has his good reasons for retreating to the Todd River. Some sites are sacred sites. The river also is one of the closest places an eager drinker can stop after buying his cheap cask of wine. The river bottoms are the easiest places for Aborigines to avoid arrest for breaking the "two-kilometer law."

Instituted in 1983 in the Northern Territory (though initiated in Alice Springs) to move Aboriginal drunkenness out of public view, the law forbids anyone to drink in a public place—meaning outdoors—within two kilometers of a pub or a store licensed to sell alcohol. The law was aimed at Aboriginal people. At the time it was written, there were only two hotels in all of Alice

Springs where they could drink. One such place was subdivided into several parts. The distinction was between a section that catered to regulars—station hands, truckers, Aborigines of mixed descent—and a tastelessly decorated room that enforced a posted notice: Patrons Are Requested To Wear Neat Attire. Then, as now, this notice can be read to mean No Aborigines Allowed. White pubs and hotels work from the assumption that Aborigines are slobs; they go everywhere barefoot, in clothes that are old and dirty. Those who don't behave according to the stereotype are taken aside by managers and bartenders and told they're not welcome.

Two hours north of Alice Springs, in the tiny roadhouse fly-through settlement of Tea-Tree, the treatment of Aborigines who wish to drink is played out in another key. One boiling Sunday afternoon I stopped in Tea-Tree to fill up on petrol and to get the cold beer I'd been thinking about for the previous hour. I took one of the high stools at the long bar, ordered a Foster's Lager, then turned to watch two Aborigines playing pool. They wobbled, looked glassy-eyed; they were drunk. Presently, I was struck by something I'd not seen before in the Centre. About as often as I took a drink from my beer an Aborigine came through a side door, handed a large beer pitcher to a bartender, fidgeted about while waiting for a refill, then disappeared through the door whence he came. A minute or two later another Aborigine went through a similar ritual.

When I finished my beer I walked through the door with the heavy traffic and came into a large enclosed yard, full of picnic tables with awnings, a trailer that had been converted into toilets, a friendly-looking wedge-tailed eagle with a badly damaged right wing, and two small red kangaroos nipping at grass. There wasn't a single white person in the yard, but there were nine or ten groups of Aborigines, each of six to eight men. Some were bunched together at the tables, others sat in circles under trees. Each group encircled two or three pitchers of beer. There was no wine nor any kind of hard alcohol.

Curious, I returned to the bar. "Why aren't they drinking wine?" I asked.

"It's their rules. That's how they want it."

"Their rules? Decided by democratic vote, or by their elders?"

"Got me, mate. Just know it's their rules and we follow them."

"Do they have other rules?"

"They can only drink here between 1:30 and 3:30 in the afternoon. Any day they want, but only in those hours."

"Where can I find the roadhouse manager?" I had doubts that I'd heard the truth, the whole story.

"He's outside, painting."

He was sitting on the ground, adding paint where it was least required, trying, I guessed, to see if he could get Tea-Tree included on an already long list of the Territory's "tidiest towns." I sought confirmation of what I'd heard earlier. The manager gave me almost identical answers. "We like it this way too," he said. "No trouble with them then. It'd be right good if it were this way all up and down the track—which it isn't."

I had another beer in the bar, then returned to the yard. The first time I hadn't noticed how many of the Aborigines were smiling. More smiles, I thought, than I'd find in a similar-sized group of whites. Several of the Aborigines from three different tables beckoned for me to join them. I went to the nearest table and took a seat on the end. I waited for my chance, then asked, "Why do you only drink beer? And why can you only drink between 1:30 and 3:30 in the afternoon?"

Heads turn toward the bar and everyone pointed. Seven thick voices sang: "That's their rule, boss. They make us do it this way."

"It's not your elders' rules?"

"No, boss," they insisted.

The statistics are staggering. Alcohol consumption is more than half again as great in The Alice as it is in the rest of Australia, and it may well exceed that of Luxembourg, which is claimed to have the highest consumption rate in the world: the equivalent of more than five gallons of pure alcohol per year for every person over fifteen. Even before the 1983 two-kilometer law came into effect, Alice accounted for almost half of all arrests for drinking in the entire Northern Territory. By contrast,

Darwin, its steamy big sister far to the north, is more than three times as large but has only one-third as many arrests for abusive drinking.

A great many whites in the Centre drink with abandon. But it is the Aborigines who have utterly dominated arrest statistics for excessive drinking. Better than eighty percent of those arrested for drunkenness in Alice Springs are Aboriginal men. A lot of this has to do with racism, the fact that Aboriginal people have not had pubs in which to drink. Aborigines have been, and still are, excluded from hotels by dress codes specifically aimed at them. A few pubs have had segregated sections for Aborigines, but many in the Territory have had no more than a "dog window" in an alley where grog could be bought. Not surprisingly, most arrests of Aborigines for drinking have taken place in public parks, even before the two-kilometer law came into effect. But however much racism has bloated arrest statistics, alcoholism has long been a problem of gigantic proportions in the Aboriginal community.

Problems with alcohol among Aboriginal people began early in the history of Australia; in fact, not long after the first ship of 750-odd British convicts dropped anchor in Botany Bay in 1788. A grotesque sport of those early penal colony days was to get Aborigines good and drunk and then cheer them on as they beat and maimed one another.

The two-kilometer law more or less had the intended effect of reducing the visibility of public drunkenness to tourists in Alice Springs. It was equally effective in increasing the amount of serious drinking in the town camps. With no other place to go, those addicted to grog took their habits home, which has resulted in more tension, more domestic squabbles, more violence. The law solved a problem for whites, at the cost of magnifying an already large one for Aborigines.

None of this has gone unnoticed by Aboriginal leaders in Alice Springs, and for several years there have been active campaigns to help Aborigines who are dependent on alcohol. One major effort is to establish social clubs where they can engage in controlled drinking and buy food and have access to detoxification, rehabilitation, educational and sobering-up programs. Aboriginal leaders want to put up four such clubs in The Alice, each strategically located to keep tensions and fighting among different groups at a minimum. There is no pretense among Aboriginal leaders that the clubs will solve the drinking problems, only that they would make it easier to control its effects.

In July of 1984 the Chief Minister of the Northern Territory, Paul Everingham, said that his government would supply land for the clubs and would match the cost of establishing them on a dollar-for-dollar basis. The offer has the appearance of being stillborn. Strong opposition has come from those who own takeaway outlets that sell alcohol to Aborigines. Were the clubs to be built, some proprietors would lose as much as five thousand dollars a week in sales.

Now there is a feeling, especially among hoteliers and liquor store owners, that the concern for tourists and town image has gone far enough. If all that money is to be lost, then surely there is nothing to be gained from a further reduction in Aboriginal visibility.

Today there are some 180,000 Aborigines in Australia. In virtually every respect they're a skewed lot when compared to national averages. Their annual income is half that of the white population, their unemployment rate four times greater, their infant mortality rate three times higher, their life expectancy twenty years lower, their proportionate representation in prisons ten times greater, and their educational level so abysmal that comparisons are all but meaningless. More than half of all Aborigines live in good-sized cities, many in slums. The rest can be found in small towns and on remote Aboriginal lands in the Outback.

No one knows exactly when Aborigines first came to a bountiful oasis in the MacDonnell Ranges that Europeans one day would name Alice Springs, but one can be sure that it was thousands of years ago. According to the most recent evidence, Aborigines have been in the Centre for at least 22,000 years; Europeans have been in residence for little more than 100. Though their hunting and gathering life precluded permanent settlement, Aborigines made frequent use of the area. It had a good supply of water and a rich array of game animals nearby. And, in Aboriginal Altjira (Dreamtime), the place that the Aranda called Mbantua became imprinted with a living geography of sacred sites.

When Europeans in 1872 etablished a telegraph station in Stuart, as Alice Springs was known until 1933, and introduced cattle to the area at about the same time, Aranda-speaking Aborigines were present in numbers far exceeding those of whites. By 1899 there were only about 30 Europeans in Alice, as compared to 150 Aborigines, most of whom were camped along the Todd and Charles rivers. Already by this time Aboriginal culture was badly disturbed, disintegrating. The anthropologist Baldwin Spencer said that

> the rapidity with which a tribe undergoes degeneration, as soon as it comes in contact with civilization, is astonishing. Disease plays havoc with its numbers; old customs are forsaken, or modified out of recognition, and beliefs that have been firmly held for ages past are quietly dropped, partly because they meet with the contempt and ridicule of the white man and partly because the young men soon learn that they are not altogether worthy of credence. Even in 1901, the condition of the Arunta tribe was very different from what it was six years earlier. . . . When I was last at Alice Springs, in 1926, not a single member of the old witchetty grub people, man, woman or child, remained alive.

Government employees who worked along the two thousand miles of telegraph line that extended from Adelaide to Darwin brought supplies for the dependent Aborigines: dresses for the women, shirts for the men, food for those who were old and unable to work. Their weekly ration was two pounds of flour, a quarter-pound of sugar, a handful of tea, and half a stick of tobacco. These rations couldn't begin to meet the needs of those most in need. By long tradition, Aborigines shared everything with their kinsmen.

By the turn of the century many Aborigines had already been rounded up from the town's hinterland and put in missions, "to

protect them against the excesses of the miners and pastoralists." The earliest mission was the German Lutheran Mission
established in 1877 at Hermannsburg, 120 kilometers west of
Alice. Travelers who passed through the mission a hundred
years ago described Aborigines much as some would describe
those in Alice Springs today.

> Nowhere on our journey did we see natives so dirty in their
> habits, so squalid in their mode of life, and so devoid of the
> usual cheery demeanor as at Hermannsburg. Altogether I
> failed to observe any features in the condition of the natives
> that might be considered evidence of an abiding improve-
> ment either mentally, morally or physically, which have
> resulted from the labours of the Missionaries. Rather the
> reverse in fact.

So to improve their sense of worth, the missionaries translated the twenty-seven books of the New Testament into Aranda
so that these desert people could recite verses. And they gave
them names, names like Matthias, Johannes, Jocabus, Daniel,
Samuel, Miriam, Rebecca, Magdalene.

Aborigines initially reacted to white settlers with curiosity,
then with fear, then with hatred as their sacred sites were dese-
crated, their best water holes lost to station homesteads, their
women raped. Aborigines fought back by spearing the white
man's cattle and filling wells along the telegraph line with rub-
bish. During the 1880s and 1890s whites retaliated with sum-
mary, often brutal justice. Aborigines were shackled, impris-
oned, mercilessly slaughtered. The constable in Alice Springs at
that time described Aborigines as "fierce and bloodthirsty, a
people who will kill and eat white men whenever they get an
opportunity. Hence it is imperative to firmly deal with the savages. . . ." The Aborigines' primitive weapons were no match for
the arsenal of steel, lead, and gunpowder possessed by the recent
arrivals.

The white settlement, composed mostly of miners (gold was
discovered in the MacDonnell Ranges in 1887) and pastoralists,
languished until 1929 when a rail line from the south was extended to the town. By 1932 there still were only 200 whites in

Alice Springs, a figure that did not grow appreciably until World War II, when the Allied military forces established a base in Alice. Twenty years later the town was given another boost, this time when the Pine Gap Research Facility was established nearby as a joint U.S.–Australian venture to monitor Soviet nuclear testing. It was at about this time, the mid 1960s, that Alice began to see its future in tourism. And take off the town did, growing in the 1960s and 1970s by as much as ten percent per year. Alice Springs still is among the fastest growing towns in Australia.

Once European hegemony was well established in Alice Springs Aborigines became "wards"; they were placed under the control of official protectors. They could not vote, they could not own land or other property, they could not legally consume alcohol, they had little freedom of movement, and everywhere they were paid much less than were whites for comparable work. Aborigines were only allowed to leave the reservations around Alice Springs if they had special permission, or if they worked in the town and remained faithful to the rule of being gone by sundown. These laws were in effect until after World War II. Only in 1967 did a national referendum give Aborigines the right to vote.

Stereotypes are commonplace. Aborigines are seen as children, and the men, whether 18 or 80, still are sometimes called boys by whites. Many believe that if you send an Aborigine out to work on his own, he'll camp under the first shady tree he comes upon. Or, as some Outback Aussies are quick to say, he'll go bush on a walkabout. Alice Springs, one will hear with a sarcastic bite, is the Australian capital of the Aboriginal rights and self-determination movement, one of the few growth areas in the Australian economy. Truth masks fear and contempt, for Alice does indeed have a number of Aboriginal organizations, and they bring in millions of dollars to the local economy from the federal government.

Early in the history of European settlement of the Centre white men were forbidden to sleep with Aboriginal women, but the law proved virtually impossible to enforce. White men outnumbered white women by better than two to one as late as 1940. But it wasn't only the familiar frontier problem of too few women that led to widespread miscegenation in the Centre. White men saw young Aboriginal women as sexually uninhibited. They would take advantage of young girls by offering them candy and biscuits to sleep with them. If they refused, the girls would be threatened with violence. Then they would be taken to the bush and given a small bag of food in return for the forced favors. Those white men who lived with Aboriginal women found them to be hard working, easily ordered about, easy to discard.

By the 1920s the Northern Territory government saw the rising number of mixed-blood children as one of its most perplexing problems: "how to check the breeding of them and how best to deal with those now with us." In one government official's mind, the issue was exacerbated because, by his preposterous calculation, Aboriginal numbers were increasing fifty times faster than whites. The concern over mixed-blood children led to a policy whereby policemen were sent out to scour the countryside in search of them. When found, children were forcibly taken from their mothers and sent to Darwin, to Alice Springs, to Adelaide. They were placed in welfare and church homes, on reserves. Girls were trained for domestic services, boys as stockmen who could then work for food and clothing rations on white cattle stations. Some officials even wanted to "breed out color" by giving mixed-blood girls the same education as white youth, which bureaucrats seemed to believe would make them attractive to marriage-minded European males.

As early as 1915 mixed-blood children were cared for and educated by the government in a corrugated iron building called The Bungalow, located behind Alice's one hotel. For a time, older girls and young women were locked in The Bungalow at night to prevent them from having sex with white men. Then, when the railroad was extended to Alice Springs in 1929, the fear of rampant "comboism," as miscegenation was called, was so great that Aboriginal women and children were moved to Jay Creek, a small settlement forty kilometers west of town. Shortly thereafter they were again moved, this time to the telegraph station northeast of Alice. A decade later, their numbers still growing, light-skinned children and their mothers were crowded into still another special reserve, known as Rainbow Town. Many made yet another move in 1960 when they were forced to move to Amoonguna, a reserve fourteen kilometers southeast of Alice.

From the earliest days of foreign occupation, Aborigines camped at the outskirts of white settlement or in the Todd River under lean-tos, behind windbreaks, in tiny humpies (bark and branch huts), in what some whites called wurleys, a native term meaning house or bird's nest. The camps were cohesive social units based on kinship ties and friendship, a common language, common geographical origins. They were set up on that side of town closest to the residents' own territorial country: the Western Aranda on the west side, the Eastern Aranda on the east side, the Walpiri and Warramungga peoples on the north side. From time immemorial the Aranda held jurisdiction over the movement of other people in and out of the Alice Springs area. For example, no one from the north or from the south was permitted to pass through Heavitree Gap without Aranda permission, a system that did not break down until the construction of alternative routes and the growth of the town's white population.

The Aboriginal town camps were seen by citizens and public officials alike as a nuisance, a public health problem, an eyesore. They were referred to by the white population as "fringe camps," judged as marginal and superfluous to the general development of the town. Until 1970 it was commonly assumed by town administrators that the town camps were largely inhabited by transient visitors, whereas in fact most of the residents had been in The Alice much longer than any of the whites.

Significant growth of the town camps began in the late 1940s, after the army withdrew and with it sources of employment and accommodation. In 1960 town officials made a concerted effort to do something about the camps and a mixed-blood population by creating a two-square-mile reserve in Amoonguna. Conditions at Amoonguna were squalid. Homes were uninsulated tin shacks of a hundred square feet each—large enough, the government declared, to house eight people.

Amoonguna became a dumping ground for people from quite different language groups and clans, which led to misunderstanding, fighting, the destruction of property. It was not an issue that attracted white attention or seemed to demand an equitable geographical solution. As late as 1977 an Alice Springs alderman voiced his desire to remove all Aborigines then congregating in Alice's town camps and in the Todd River, dump them at Amoonguna, and encircle the reserve with a high wire fence to keep them in.

Today, Amoonguna is freehold Aboriginal land. A once-thriving business in brick-making is now only a memory. The overwhelming majority of Amoonguna's Aborigines are on the dole. The few local sources of employment include garbage collection services and Aboriginal organizations. A mixture of Walpiri and Eastern Aranda peoples once inhabited Amoonguna, but most of the Walpiri have left or been forced out. This more or less solved the problem of disparate clans with different traditions.

In the last ten years the population of Amoonguna has remained steady at about 300, but the amount of housing has been considerably reduced. After Amoonguna became freehold Aboriginal land in the late 1970s, several of the houses were sold to whites for a pittance when quick money was needed. Through the years others were trashed or destroyed when an elder died and sons and daughters couldn't decide who should have control of the house. Today only twenty-four houses remain in the community. The prospects for new housing are bleak.

Leadership in Amoonguna is minimal, and this is made worse by a community population that is constantly in flux. The large population of Eastern Aranda who live in the much larger freehold Aboriginal community of Santa Teresa to the southeast use Amoonguna as a way station on visits to Alice Springs.

Under the Social Welfare Ordinance of 1964, Aborigines gained the freedom to drink like everyone else, to have sexual relations with members of other races, and—at least in theory—to live where they would. It was 1968 before Aborigines who worked on pastoral properties received the same wages as whites, and it was another eight years before a federal Aboriginal Land Rights Act—applicable only to the Northern Territory—allowed Australia's blacks to claim unalienated public land, or that not wanted or used by others.

The 1976 Land Rights Act came none too soon for Alice's blacks. At that time a survey found that a thousand town campers had access to ten showers, eleven toilets, and no electrical outlets. Only two of the then nearly two dozen town camps were legal in the eyes of white administrators. The others were composed of illegal squatters, subject to eviction at any time.

By the early 1970s there were so many Aborigines in Alice's town camps they could no longer be ignored. They applied for leases on crown land in the town, but more often than not their petitions were denied. They were denied on the grounds that their requests were not "rational." Finally, in 1975, after an intensive legal investigation, Aborigines were given blocks of land chosen by them. This was then ratified by the Land Rights Act. The Act didn't guarantee, however, that leases would be granted expeditiously. By 1983 a third of Alice Spring's eighteen town camps still did not have legal ninety-nine year leases. Uncertainty of tenure and lack of access to the most basic services have been magnified by monstrous poverty, a ninety percent unemployment rate, and the lack of sufficient housing.

Unlike the extremely fluid white population, the 1,200 to 1,500 town campers have spent the greater part of their lives in The Alice. And yet town camp numbers frequently swell, doubling, sometimes tripling. This results from the influx of visitors from Aboriginal-owned lands, from cattle stations, from distant bush communities known as outstations. People who speak Pitjantjatjara, Yuankunytjara, Alyawarra, Warumungu, Anmatyerre, Warlmanpa come to Alice to renew kinship bonds, to participate in important rituals, to marry in defiance of prescribed kinship rules, to drink. After a while they leave again. The white concept of a household as a fixed number of people just doesn't work for the Aborigine.

Not all Aborigines who have tried to make Alice home have found themselves socially and geographically excluded. Indeed, Alice's 3,500 or so Aborigines fall into two principal groups:

those who are town campers and wish to live in relatively homogeneous units and reject European values, and those with lifestyles not much different from those of many whites. Many in the latter group are part-Aborigines who live in conventional or government-subsidized housing, were educated in public schools, speak English as their principal language, and share many white Australian values. Despite apparent material success, many mixed bloods who do not wish to deny their past find themselves in that lumpy netherland where social discourse is difficult, no matter which way they turn.

I read in the paper that an Aboriginal man was given a $600 fine by an Alice Springs judge for being caught with alcohol on Utopia. Utopia is a failed Aboriginal cattle station several hours north of Alice. The convicted man and several friends had planned to go to a creek bed, get drunk, and stay there until the effects wore off.

Like several large and small black settlements in the Centre, Utopia is dry. In virtually every case, the decision to prohibit alcohol was made by community elders. They have wanted to rid their communities of drunkenness and frequent fights and wife beatings, get their people to spend their money on food and other necessities rather than on a drug that is killing them.

In handing down his decision, the white judge noted that Papunya, an Aboriginal settlement three hours west of Alice Springs, had declared itself dry several years ago. Since then there have been no deaths attributable to drunken brawls. Prior to that time, the community of several hundred people was averaging four a year.

WHEN RABBITS
RUN WILD

As soon as we pass through the station gate and over the cattle grid, my eyes are drawn to healthy patches of camel weed, wire grass, and yellow-flowered broombrush, unpalatable plants that quickly multiply on overgrazed land. Presently, I notice that the iron-rich dirt track we're shaking over in a four-wheel-drive Land Rover is running parallel to two deep-set gullies. Pointing, I turn to Graham Pearce, the Commonwealth Scientific and Industrial Research Organization scientist who's my host. "What's happened here?"

"Former vehicle tracks. One goes, then you move over ten or fifteen yards and cut another one. That one goes and you do the same again." He explains that with several seasons of periodic rains, the tracks quickly pass through a predictable succession of stages: from coarse sandpaper surfaces to deepening rivulets to wind- and water-washed canyons good for little more than classroom examples of human-induced soil erosion. Graham shakes his head in disgust and mumbles about how the road should have been graded.

Graham is one of two biologists with CSIRO who have been conducting experiments since 1981 to sort out the effects of rabbits on vegetation in central Australia. He makes frequent night visits to Owen Springs station, a 1,400-square-mile cattle station south of Alice Springs. Graham carries out spotlight counts of rabbits, whose numbers vary from zero to seven hundred per square kilometer, depending on food and rainfall. He also monitors two different experimental enclosures, one of which is rabbit proof. Over a six-year period in the rabbit-proof enclosure, witchetty bush and palatable grasses have increased from zero to densities that would allow for grazing of three cows per square kilometer, about the maximum carrying capacity of this particular land when in good condition.

Despite a long history of devastation caused by rabbits in Australia, no systematic study of their effect on land grazed by cattle in the Centre had been done as late as 1978. In spite of all kinds of undeniable evidence, about all that scientists in the Centre could agree on was that rabbits were "probably" having a significant effect on the cattle industry, and "probably" destroying native flora and fauna.

We drive on a bit farther and another feature brakes my eyes. Everywhere witchetty bushes and mulga are naked of leaves up to more than two meters. Witchetty bush and mulga, both common in the Centre, are considered topfeed by cattlemen. Topfeed is a reserve source of food; it constitutes as much as ten to fifteen percent of livestock diet, two to three times this much on stations badly overstocked. You expect to see plenty of browsed branches when there's been no significant rain for some time. But when you can hold a surveyor's string above your head under long lines of mulga and witchetty bush—even ironwoods and whitewoods—and not touch a leaf, it's fair to conclude that either times have been very bad or there are far too many hungry mouths around.

History shows that cattlemen in the Centre frequently have overstocked their stations in years with lots of rain. When dry times came they cut down mulga and other edible trees in the hope of saving starving livestock.

"Station owners around here don't know how to read their land," Graham says. "Around here they read the condition of their property by looking at the livestock. If the cattle aren't losing weight, then everything must be all right. But when the cattle start to look bad, it's already too late. By then the land's flogged and the serious damage has already been done. It's easier that way. You tell them to do it the other way around, that it'll make for better turn-off rates and higher profits in the long run, they tell you to get stuffed."

On we bump over the neglected station road, initial readings of some larger problem coming into focus. Ahead, in shade under bloodwood and prickly wattle, I see a small mob of Herefords. Shorthorns are dominant in this part of the Centre, but Herefords are on the increase. They walk better and they're more resistant to drought, admirable qualities where rainfall is unpredictable, palatable grasses in short supply, the land neglected.

The Herefords are now almost close enough to touch. They're bony, a long long way from market weight. Six weeks earlier there was a drenching rainfall, seven inches in all. In the ensuing weeks there was more rain, a total amount well in excess of the norm for this part of the Centre. But it was the wrong kind of rain; it wasn't what they call a "seed rain," one that comes in the warmer months and produces weighty grasses that put on kilos of beef.

Another four kilometers into the station we break into a vast clearing that clears my mind of all previous impressions. All the way to the purple and brick-red MacDonnell Ranges, I stare in disbelief at a huge arena that looks scorched, desolate, virtually dead. There are no trees or shrubs—no living trees or shrubs, I mean. Every last mulga and witchetty bush is leafless, black and brown and brittle, down.

"How long have these trees been dead?" I ask.

"Some thirty, forty years. What you see has come on over a long time." He adjusts his glasses, plows a sun-weathered hand through his greying hair, and goes into high gear. He informs me that I'm looking at a complex puzzle. How do you weigh or measure all the possible causes and culprits? Drought, fire, too many cattle, too many feral horses, too many rabbits. Man.

Drought, from a station owner's point of view, is always easy to implicate. Blame the ransacked vegetation, the dying cows, the bulging mortgage, the declining income on another "unusual" year, a year without "adequate" rainfall. Never blame it on overgrazing, bad management practices, feral horses you seldom see, rabbits you don't care about.

Accessibility to diffuse water is another problem. Just about anything within several kilometers of a dam or water trough is heavily grazed. Graham opines that savvy station owners not afraid of blemishing their macho image use plastic piping to locate water among plants not favored by livestock. "A good rule of thumb is to choose a site about five kilometers from the most favored plant communities. Site your bore in mulga. That way, you save your feed and your best soils. A little good management, reading the land, that's all we're talking about."

When healthy, limestone soils are highly productive, a condition known as sweet country. Sweet country produces well-finished livestock. Good calcareous soils nurture thick carpets of succulent forbs and delicious grasses: oat grass, kerosene grass, mulga grass, others. These grasses, like water, bring in not only cattle but all kinds of hungry beasts: red kangaroos, untamed donkeys, feral horses, rabbits. The good feed attracts rabbits by the thousands. They go first for the water-soaked forbs, then for the grasses, then for the leaves and bark of trees. Soon ringbarking is underway; the bark provides just enough moisture to make it edible, but the bark has so little nutrient value that the rabbits actually die of starvation while simultaneously killing the trees. Even when rabbits can't be blamed for denuding a landscape, in large numbers they're responsible for preventing trees from returning. As soon as seedlings appear, they devour them.

Early nineteenth-century explorers who passed through this part of the Centre noted the profusion of grasses. The now rare small wallaby leaped out from under their horses' hooves. The Horn Expedition of 1894 took note of rabbit-eared bandicoots, said that "their burrows abounded." A quarter of a century later the bandicoots would be gone; rabbits would be living in their homes.

Graham stops on a humpy moonscape, shuts off the engine, and leans forward onto the steering wheel. He sighs and says, "Besides rabbits, now way down, there's bugger-all here."

I get out of the truck and walk around. Here and there I come on rabbit warrens with twenty, thirty, forty entrances. Graham comes up beside me, hunches over, points to runways into the warrens. "They're not here yet," he says, pointing to the dry ground, no sign of recent droppings anywhere. "But they'll come, you got no worries there, mate."

After a couple of seasons of good rains there can be as many as two hundred such openings in these vast breeding grounds. In ever-enlarging circles around the warrens I see little more than walnut-sized islands of crusty dirt supporting the merest hint of edible grass. Here and there are clumps of bluebush and salt-bush, which neither cattle nor rabbits care for because of the high salt content. Highly productive soil, once abundant, has been washed into crevices, low spots, oblivion. The earth is pebbly, clayey, cemented. It acts like wax paper when it rains. Six inches of rain can fall on these badly eroded surfaces and hardly any of it will soak into the ground. Since there is so little infiltration, mulga and witchetty bush cannot grow, even if rabbits are not around to eat the seedlings.

I jump ahead in the story and ask Graham, "Can some of this land be reclaimed?"

"Yeah, it can. With buffel grass."

Buffel grass probably was brought into central Australia by cameleers in the nineteenth century. It spread along creeks and river banks and soon colonized the most productive plant communities. A strong, aggressive, deep-rooting perennial that is drought-hearty, frost-resistant, and can withstand persistent heavy grazing, buffel grass will grow on virtually all major soil types in the Centre. The grass grows rapidly and seeds often; when it rains, buffel grass is exceptionally high in protein and gives a reasonably good quantity of biomass. Even so, buffel grass won't fatten cattle nearly as well as a poor-quality native grass.

Once buffel grass has been planted it's almost impossible to displace. Once on the scene, its future as a viable species is akin to that of rabbits, horses, pigs, cats, the dreaded *Mimosa pigra* now sweeping through Kakadu National Park. Were a disease deadly to buffel grass to find its way into the Centre, then, as has happened with introduced grasses elsewhere in Australia, fields of plenty would be reduced to landscapes as barren of food as are those of the forbidding sand dunes of the Simpson Desert.

Buffel grass came to prominence after the prolonged dry period of the 1960s. Because it is useful for reclaiming worn-out land, more than six thousand square kilometers of pasture was covered with the grass by the late 1970s. Today the Conservation Commission will supply buffel grass to cattle station owners free of charge, even plant it. But the owner and the manager of the station we're on, Owen Springs station, want nothing to do with the grass.

"Why not?" I ask.

"Who knows. Could be any reason you can imagine."

We drive farther out onto the arresting skateboard devastation; to my left is the rounded lip of a dam, in another direction scores of emaciated cattle carcasses, food for dingoes, feral cats, wedge-tailed eagles. The cattle, I learn, were in bad shape when the nearby dam went dry. The station manager hoped, as so many of them hope in the Centre, that their stock would be saved by rain. The rain came. But when it came it was like administering last rites to animals all but legally dead.

The longer I look at this horror before me, the more it reminds me of a spooky landscape in a Mad Max movie. But the analogy, I realize, has a fatal flaw; much of central Australia is not the desert people glibly portray it to be. A rainfall chart for this area shows that every year between 1973 and 1978 had at least fifteen inches of precipitation. Three years had more than twenty; 1974 had thirty-one. Not a single year in the 1970s had less than four inches, the amount that falls on what is often taken as the northern limit of the Sahara Desert.

Still, the Centre is arid, and like all arid lands there is considerable fluctuation around a rainfall mean. From 1958 to 1966 central Australia experienced one of the worst droughts on record. During those eight years rainfall exceeded ten inches only twice. Only three inches fell in 1965. Pastoralists had no choice but to drastically reduce cattle numbers, from 360,000 to 130,000 in the southern half of the Territory.

There is no required maximum stocking rate on leased public land in the Northern Territory. Early in the Territory's history the government established a minimum rate only. This was done to ensure that the land was used and to prevent land speculation, frenetic buying and selling by investors. After the government's first Northern Territory land sale in 1863, most of the 723 buyers demanded their money back within a few years. Soon thereafter the government offered free passage to anyone from Japan and India who would settle in the Territory. No one was interested.

By the early 1880s, however, there was a spectacular boom, as Australians and foreigners alike rushed to secure pastoral leases. Many who filed applications had never set food on antipodean soil. By 1883 more than ninety percent of the Territory had been applied for, considerably more than was held a hundred years later. Enthusiasm for exploiting the land was real enough; by the 1880s there already were more than 60,000 head of cattle in the Territory. The first shipments of frozen beef and mutton went to England in 1879. With visions of a bottomless overseas market, pastoralists allowed cattle numbers to increase in good years well beyond what the land could carry. Serious overgrazing occurred, and henceforth it would continue to occur largely without interruption. Overgrazing was abetted by the voracious appetites of absentee landlords, many of whom lived abroad. The stations were run by managers whose mandate was to maximize short-term profits.

Maximum stocking rates frequently have been discussed and advocated by scientists and conservationists in the Centre, but the discussions have gone nowhere. Pastoralists have long maintained that a stocking rate that's appropriate in one year will be way out of kilter the following year, when precipitation is double or half the norm. This is a fair enough argument, one easily buttressed by the variable carrying capacity of the land; on a square kilometer basis, it can vary from less than half a cow to more than eight. Still, pastoralists make exaggerated use of their freedom. When there's been a string of good years they run more than 400,000 cows on the ninety or so stations that spread like a broken fan around Alice Springs. In really good years, the figure is upwards of 500,000. Scientists feel that to keep the land healthy you need to halve these numbers. And they're not taking into account feral horses; if they were, the number of cattle would have to be reduced by seventy percent or more.

There is, as it happens, a Northern Territory Conservation and Land Utilization Act that was meant to protect the land from human-induced degradation. The Act specifies that if soil erosion can be proved, a station owner can be prosecuted, even lose his lease. But the ordinance has no meaning. No one in the government has been willing to try to quantify soil erosion, or, to put the matter differently, to do so and then argue a case for abusive management in a court of law. Station owners have immense influence. Or at least they're alleged to have such power; scientists don't test this proposition the way they do all their other hypotheses.

Graham mentions that hard as it has been to bring about positive change on Owen Springs station and many similar stations, it may be even harder in the future. The station is one of a handful in the Territory that recently has been granted a perpetual lease. The perpetual lease was granted because of recent changes in land management, the addition of new bores and fences in the mid 1970s. It was not granted, could not have been granted, on the basis of previous practices. Indeed, the station's 1,400 square miles have been subjected to massive abuses for the better part of a century.

Perpetual leases recently have come into vogue with pastoralists in central Australia. Unlike common leases that run for periods of thirty-five to fifty years in the Territory, a perpetual lease is little more than a blinking yellow light just down the street from freehold. In concrete terms, a perpetual lease means that a station owner will be able to pursue his every whim, more or less with impunity. Station owners want perpetual leases for a variety of reasons: because they believe that it will be easier to use the station as collateral on bank loans; because a perpetual lease will make a station look better, more saleable; simply because Aborigines are now being given freehold title (in trust, not to individuals) in the Territory and, therefore, why shouldn't whites, who own all but a handful of stations in the Territory, have the same rights? Whatever reason a particular station owner gives for wanting a perpetual lease, once one is in place there may be no chance for government agencies to offer advice on how and when to control feral animals and plaguing rabbits.

Australia is infamous for its exotic pests, most of all for the wild English rabbit. Rabbits were introduced in 1859 when Thomas Austin, a squatter who lived near Geelong, Victoria, released twenty-four of them for sport. He did so, he said, because "we are so destitute to the means of enjoying country life. There is nothing here in the way of game for people of sporting proclivities and I have always found these animals to be a most desirable element in the community." By 1865 Austin, who loved to record his shooting feats in Victorian newspapers, had shot 20,000 rabbits on his property. Two years later the rabbit figure was above 34,000.

As Thomas Austin quickly discovered, rabbits do indeed breed like rabbits. A female can become pregnant at three months of age and produce twenty-five young before a year has gone by, the same year in which her daughters and granddaughters also will be tending their young.

Australia proved to be a paradise for the profligate breeder. The winters were mild, the rivers were bordered by sweet green feed, and there were plenty of enticing woodlands and sandy hills in which to burrow and reproduce. By 1880 rabbits had reached the Murray River between Victoria and New South Wales. Six years later they crossed the Queensland border, five years after that they were sighted in South Australia, and by 1907 they were reported on Australia's west coast.

In 1901 the anthropologists Baldwin Spencer and F. J. Gillen, who did intensive research on the Aborigines of the Centre, found that women made ample use of rabbits when making body ornaments. The skins also were used for water bags. The animal was cut open at the throat, the skin was turned back until the front legs were skinned to the joint, and then the feet were pushed through the skin of the upper part of the leg. This sort of process was continued until the animal was completely skinned, particular attention being given to keeping all the holes as small as possible. The openings, with the exception of the one at the neck, were pinned together with a rabbit's rib bone and a fur string. The skin was then blown up through the neck opening, the hair singed off, and the bag cleansed with a fluid made from the acacia bark. After a couple of hours the bag was ready to be used. Although whites thought the bags useless because the water often turned putrid after a short while, this was of no consequence to Aborigines.

After Aborigines overcame their initial suspicions about this amazing newcomer into their environment, which they described as a tchungoo—a rat kangaroo—with ears like a donkey and a tail thought to be like that of a nanny goat, they eagerly incorporated the rabbit into their diet. When rabbit numbers were up, Aboriginal women, often with the assistance of dogs and perhaps of a young or old man who wasn't working on a cattle station, would have no trouble catching a dozen or more in a day. They would take their catch back to the hearth and, as with rats and snakes, cook them whole, guts and all, over a fire. They believed that if an animal had been opened prior to cooking its meat would be spoiled. It would be a while before Aborigines would begin to disdain rabbit meat, preferring instead virtually anything that was native to their country.

By 1902 an expedition into the Musgrave Ranges, on the border between South Australia and the Northern Territory, claimed that rabbits were swarming all over the mountains. Already by this time there were staggering reports of millions of them elsewhere in Australia. In a single night tens of thousands could be killed against fences during a rabbit drive or poisoned around a single water hole. By the turn of the century more than twenty million had been destroyed in New South Wales alone.

In their invasion of the Centre, rabbits developed their highways alongside inland salt lakes and water systems where there were rich and dependable food supplies. They followed the Finke and the Hay and the Plenty rivers, the ancient river systems from Lake Amadeus to Lake Mackay. Only in places like the forbidding Simpson Desert was the diffusion of rabbits slowed.

What is most phenomenal about the pestiferous invasion is the rate at which the wily animals diffused into the heart of the

Australian continent, on average more than 300 kilometers per year. This compares with about 112 kilometers in New South Wales, 130 for Western Australia, and 70 for Australia as a whole. Part of this notable difference can be accounted for by above-average rainfall in the years before the drought of 1899–1902. Part of it is attributable to the effective elimination of Outback predators. Hunting gentlemen of the time were enthusiastic poisoners. They much loved the "proper use of strychnine," especially for any creature that might seem troublesome to domestic animals: the wedge-tailed eagle, the dingo, the goanna. Too, much of the vegetative cover of the Centre was yet to be drastically altered by European grazing practices. Rabbits apparently needed no help from man as they radiated northward. Unlike elsewhere in Australia, where geographical spread was aided by travelers, trappers, and tramps who took along live rabbits in baskets and billy cans and turned them loose, there is no evidence of this practice in the Centre.

The rabbit may well have been the greatest single tragedy to befall Australia's arid and semi-arid lands. Examination of pre-European skeletal remains suggests there were many more species of small mammals in the Centre than anyone had ever realized. Among other misfortunes, the burrows of the greater bilby and the burrowing bettong were ready-made homes for the rabbit.

Rabbits probably reached their maximum distribution in central Australia by the mid 1920s. Since then, drought and myxomatosis have reduced their range. Today rabbits are patchily distributed, with their largest concentrations in calcareous shrubby grasslands, on fringings and dunes, and on sandy stream frontage south of Alice Springs. In good years rabbits occur in plague numbers—more than seven hundred per square kilometer is not uncommon on some cattle stations—while in dry years they almost disappear. In the Centre rabbits have reached these horde densities at least once in every decade since the turn of the century, and in twenty of the last ninety years.

Rabbits rose to plague proportions in the Centre in 1983 and again in 1985. It usually requires only three successive seasons—

two winters and the intervening summer—of good rains for rabbits to reach densities in excess of 600 per square kilometer.

Myxomatosis, caused by a deadly virus introduced intentionally in 1950 and which quickly reduced rabbit numbers by more than ninety percent in many areas of Australia, needs a suitable insect vector to work effectively. It appears that a vector, a transmitting agent that works well in temperate and humid climes, such as the European rabbit flea, may not be nearly so successful in arid environments. Following the big drought of the 1960s, myxomatosis was not reported again in rabbit populations in the Centre until 1973. The exact reason for its disappearance is not known, although the long drought may virtually have annihilated both the host and vector populations. Also, genetic resistance to myxomatosis may still be increasing, which means that even if a good drought-resistant insect is found it may not be able to do what's required.

To complicate the picture further, station owners rarely attempt to eradicate this pest when there is a drought and the population is low, which would be the ideal time to strike. Pastoralists simply don't look very far ahead. They are blind to the idea that the lower the population base the longer it takes rabbits to reach plague proportions.

The size of cattle stations, the high costs of labor, the up-and-down rabbit populations, and the animal's wide range combine to make ripping and fumigating warrens and using poisons unattractive to most stockmen. Nor is shooting by professional rabbit hunters very effective. One reason, in itself usually sufficient to negate its value, is that it is in the shooter's best interest not to kill young rabbits. Otherwise, he'll quickly put himself out of business.

Graham Pearce believes that the cheapest and most effective solution is to blow up the warrens. He may or may not be right. The method is little tested and it could be hard to convince conservative station owners of its efficacy, at least as hard as it is to shape their perspective on the dingo, the wild dog that came to Australia some three to four thousand years ago from Southeast Asia.

Aborigines regarded dingoes as pets and companions, and children slept with them at night to keep warm. Women suckled the pups; with a sharp sense of smell, the twenty-five to thirty-five pound adult semi-domesticated dogs then made sharp distinctions between local tribal members and foreigners. When Europeans came to Australia and brought along their pets, the ginger and black and tan four-foot-long descendants of Asian pale-footed wolves bred freely with Irish terriers, fox terriers, and other domestic counterparts.

Once white settlers perceived the dingo as a threat to livestock—in the occasional calf killed, in the scarifying wound marks on domestic animals' hind legs—they got the government to establish a bounty system to eliminate them. Bounties were initiated in central Australia in 1924, somewhat earlier elsewhere. Aborigines, who killed many more dingoes than whites did, often exchanged scalps for little more than flour and tobacco, for a fraction of their real value. In the 1920s an Aborigine might receive a one-pound bag of flour for eighty or ninety dead dingoes. In the early part of this century dingo scalps were a kind of currency among some Aboriginal tribes of the Centre, just as beaver skins played that role in the territories of the Hudson's Bay Company.

Aboriginal doggers—the name given to those who hunted dingoes—were famous for their ability to find the animals. They knew the whereabouts of the best patches of open sandy country where the dogs hunted in winter, and they were intimately familiar with permanent surface water in the mountains where dingoes concentrated in summer. Dingoes need water more often than do most marsupials, once a day in the summer. One consequence of this is that the provision of water for livestock increased dingo numbers well beyond what they were before the arrival of Europeans.

Pups were the chief targets of doggers. The same bounty was paid for a pup as for an adult, and the amount of time required to track and spear a single adult was as great or greater than that required to locate a litter, which included from four to eight pups. Too, Aborigines quickly came to appreciate that it was not in their best interest to kill bitches.

Dingoes were killed by shooting, trapping, and poisoning, the latter being by far the most common and successful method. One favorite routine for poisoning was to use fat from the hump of a camel. Cut into cubes and laced with strychnine, the camel fat had the virtue of not melting in the intense Outback heat. Aborigines also liked to mix strychnine into a sardine tin or impregnate kangaroo meat with a poison and then bury it just below the surface of the ground. Trapping invariably proved less effective than poisoning, and more often than not was unusually inhumane. Dingoes, desperate to get free, would sometimes gnaw off a leg to free themselves from steel traps. Some doggers would lash up to half a dozen rifles to trees near water holes. The rifles were sighted at dingo height, and a wire tied to the trigger was stretched across a known dingo track.

Like wolves in North America, dingoes have received an unusual amount of attention from governments and others intent on eradication. Nor have Outback cattlemen been any less eager to kill them. Better than eighty percent of cattlemen in the Centre today poison dingoes. No other unwanted four-footed animal receives anything like this concern from station owners.

To be sure, dingoes do occasionally attack and eat calves and wound the hindquarters of cattle. Sometimes, particularly when excessively hungry, they may roam in packs and maim and kill several calves. But based on studies done in numerous parts of arid and semi-arid Australia, rabbits constitute half or more of a dingo's diet. Whatever beef a dingo eats comes largely from carrion, except during a bad drought. Most of the time dingoes complement their diet of rabbit and carrion with rodents, kangaroos, lizards, birds, insects. The perceived significance of dingoes in reducing cattlemen's profits in Outback Australia is much overdrawn in comparison to the damage caused by poor management practices, livestock diseases, and large feral animals.

Owen Springs is one of the oldest stations in the Northern Territory. By 1873 more than 1,500 head of cattle, driven north from South Australia, grazed on the property. Two years later the station was declared adequately stocked by the government and a lease was issued. By the 1880s a new owner was running 1,800 thoroughbred hacks, most for sale to the Indian army. Horsebreeding for the Indian remount program and the Commonwealth military forces would continue until the First World War. Many of the horses became feral, thereby initiating another major problem.

Owen Springs changed hands a number of times in the decades around the turn of the century. By the early 1930s the station's land was in miserable condition. For too long there had been inconstant tenancy, lack of fences, sole dependence on natural surface waters, and far too many cattle for the available feed—on the order of 8,000 to 10,000 head at times. It was only in the mid 1970s, when yet another owner took over, that the number of dams and wells was significantly increased and paddocks were fenced.

Several weeks after my visit to Owen Springs station with Graham Pearce, I drive out to the homestead. I find the station manager, John Brumbie, in the machine shed. He's wearing faded blue jeans, an old cotton long-sleeve shirt, elastic-band R. M. Williams boots, a wide-brimmed hat. He greets me offhandedly. Before coming, I'd had trouble convincing him that he should take some time to talk with me about station management. He doesn't like troublemakers, which means outsiders—any outsiders.

After some pleasantries we talk about his spread. He says that he runs all Herefords because they bring the most at market. He explains that he wants a freehold lease so he can sell pieces of the station as opportunity dictates.

As the conversation starts to die I tell him I've seen the CSIRO experimental enclosures to keep out rabbits.

"Impressive the damage those rabbits do," I say.

"That happened because about eight years ago we had a drought and a hailstorm and then lots of rabbits."

"What do you think of the experiments?"

"Bloody damn thing, those enclosures! Can't be trusted. Now they're talking about going elsewhere with some of that work. I told them, 'Stay here and give me the results. You started here, finish here.'"

"Why do you poison dingoes?"

"What do you mean, why do I poison them?"

"Don't dingoes keep down your rabbit population?" I mention Allambi station, a hundred kilometers to the southeast. There the owner poisons dingoes on the eastern side of the station, where he has few rabbits, but leaves them alone on the western side, where rabbits are abundant.

"Don't know about that. You ever see a dingo take down a calf?"

"No."

He vividly describes a dingo biting a helpless calf on the hind legs, then tells me how a pack of dingoes, some crossed with large mongrels and Alsatians that have wandered away from their Aboriginal masters on the northern boundary of the station, will attack a full-grown cow. He's seen it happen many times, he assures me. Then he says that a dingo will only eat one rabbit a day, that it would take a stadium full of them to control rabbits when their numbers go berserk.

"How many calves do you lose in a year?"

"Don't keep figures."

"Can you give me an estimate?"

I don't get an answer. John Brumbie turns to an assistant, tells him to check the transmission oil.

"I see that you lost seventy-five or a hundred head of cattle near the dam."

"Yeah, I tried to get them out of there but couldn't do it fast enough. The water dried up and they died. It's happened before."

"Are you doing anything to control the brumbies I saw at the dam?"

For the first time, he asks what my real business is, exactly where I stand on the horses. "You love them ugly things, too?" he growls.

"If you can't muster the horses and you've got a lot of them around, then I'm for shooting them."

He cracks a smile, gives the first strong hint that we're members of the same species, maybe even the same tribe. He lets me know what he thinks about "bloody greenies," overeager conservationists. I don't react, and he says, "No, I haven't shot any horses to speak of in the areas where rabbits are a problem. There aren't that many of them. Anyway, bullets are expensive."

Who knows? In a year or two John Brumbie might try to muster them when there are enough to make it worthwhile. In the northwest section of the station it's another matter, he finally tells me. Between 1980 and 1983 he shot more than 2,000 horses there. He says they were eating everything on the ground that resembled food, leaving nothing for his cattle. He doesn't tell me that he'd been prodded by the Department of Primary Production and the Conservation Commission to do something about his feral horse problem. He does say that there are still horses in that section of the station that ought to be eliminated, but that he won't do anything because adjoining station managers aren't doing anything about their feral horses. "So I shoot mine, then I get theirs coming over."

A side effect of the shooting, one that John Brumbie doesn't mention, is that the precise area where the horses roamed and fed at will is richly endowed with rare and relict species, some of them endangered. Most occur in secluded gorges. They may be secure from cattle. It is less certain that some of the plants survived the keen foraging habits of the more adventuresome and wide-ranging feral horses.

I turn the conversation back to rabbits and dingoes. John Brumbie explains that he, like other cattlemen, occasionally calls in the Conservation Commission to poison the wild dogs. Dingoes are recognized as a native species in the Northern Territory. They supposedly are protected under a Territory and Parks Wildlife Conservation Act of 1980. In point of fact, it's always open season on dingoes outside Arnhem Land, which belongs to Aborigines.

The Commission's method is simple, John Brumbie explains. He shoots a brumby or an old steer that's not going to bring much at market, cuts it up into chunks, spikes it with a lethal injection of a poison called 1080 (sodium monofluroacetate), and then drops the poisoned bait around wells and along creeks where there's water. The poison is one of the most toxic substances known, but it has several virtues to recommend its use. Birds and many Australian marsupials are apparently immune to 1080; a variant of the poison occurs naturally in some plants these animals eat. Small doses of 1080 are highly lethal to dingoes, and the poison degrades quickly in the environment. Regardless of 1080's perceived virtues, when John Brumbie finds a calf that's been attacked by a dingo he wastes no time waiting for the Conservation Commission to find a place on its calendar for him. Right away he takes out his cache of strychnine and sprinkles a good quantity of it all over the victim.

"I get seven or eight dingoes every time," he says.

Strychnine has long been used in Australia to poison "vermin," any sort of animal or insect that gets in the way of making money from farming or livestock. Some years ago it became necessary to get a license to use strychnine, because of the belated realization that it can have a devastating effect on wildlife. But John Brumbie can do without such government regulations, thanks. He stashed away a good supply of it when he saw that times were changing. He knows what strychnine can do. He lets me know that you can't be as certain about products not tested by long experience.

The test of time is one of the reasons John Brumbie is against the proposal of the Conservation Commission and the Department of Primary Production to plant buffel grass on his station to reduce soil erosion, save land, provide an additional source of feed.

"That grass might take over my natives. Another thing. I was moving my cows along one day and saw they were only taking the heart out of the buffel grass and leaving the rest."

Owen Springs station is home to more than 160 native species, including some rare ones, such as ghost bats and rock rats. And others not so rare but nice to have around: emus, Australian kestrels, brown falcons, bustards, button-quail, diamond doves, willy wagtails, ring-necked parrots, red-tailed black cockatoos, red kangaroos, euros. Owen Springs is very close to two of the largest and more important national parks in the Centre, Simpson Gorge National Park and Finke River National Park. I'm tempted to ask John Brumbie if he knows how strychnine behaves in nature's food chain, if he thinks that animals know where the park boundaries end and his station fences begin. But I don't. I know that even some scientists with the Conservation Commission aren't particularly concerned about the use of the poison. It'll kill some wedge-tailed eagles, and a few other raptors, they say. But we've got plenty of them, so why worry?

This cavalier attitude toward the wedge-tailed eagle is rationalized in part by looking at contemporary relationships between man and other animals in central Australia. Abundant livestock carrion, rabbits, and feral cats are at the top of a rather lengthy list of animals that provide ample food for eagles. In spite of the fact that two decades ago as many as 30,000 wedge-tails a year were being killed in Australia, they're abundant in the Centre, and by all measures their numbers are increasing.

What's wrong with a relaxed attitude is not just that eagles are a native form of life that ought to be preserved, not just that other less abundant animal life is destroyed by strychnine, but also the fact that the eagles are known to have an appetite for rabbits. Where wedge-tailed eagle diets have been studied, between forty and ninety-eight percent of their diet is composed of rabbits. Admittedly, their impact on large populations is small; on the other hand, when rabbit numbers are down, as during a drought, the eagles inhibit their post-drought recovery.

I make one last effort to get John Brumbie to tell me how he sees dingoes, how his cost-benefit calculations are made. But I can't seem to find just the right question to draw him out. From the tone of how he'd talked about dingoes and lost calves, however, I think I understand that the sight of so many dollars lost to an easily identified predator like the dingo is palpable in a way that the arguments of scientists on the damage caused by rabbits are not.

Among scientists who collectively have spent decades in the Centre researching the relationship between dingoes and rabbits, there is more than a little hemming and hawing. One argument goes something like this. If you have a rabbit problem, then dingoes may be desirable enough to leave them alone, even if you're losing some small percentage of calves, even, possibly, if a bountiful diet of rabbit meat is increasing the dingo population. But if rabbits begin to approach plague proportions, when profound and sometimes irreversible damage is done, then it's quite unlikely that you're going to have anywhere near enough dingoes to take care of the problem. Of course, during a rabbit plague dingoes don't need to eat calves.

If you try to decimate your dingo population because of drought and the fact that the rabbits have crashed, perhaps not realizing that dingoes in large numbers do reduce a moderately sized rabbit population, then with a couple of seasons of good rains you might find yourself with more rabbits than you imagined possible. CSIRO scientists have estimated that rabbits increase four times faster when dingoes are eliminated. Now you have a "predator" of a different sort to worry about, one that has a determined predilection for grass kept short and palatable, just the way cattle keep it. One hundred rabbits eat as much as one cow. If the density of rabbits is 700 per square kilometer and a station is carrying seven cows per square kilometer and livestock numbers are at carrying capacity, then the land, in effect, is being double-stocked.

In the rabbit you have an animal that at high densities increases the presence of annual grasses and reduces the available forage in subsequent growth cycles. You have a meaty creature that furnishes feral cats and foxes with an additional source of food, and increases these populations, which feed on native wildlife. The rabbit, with its sharp, chisel-like teeth, will kill a tree by gnawing through the bark to reach the juicy vascular tissue. When there's a drought and rabbits are abundant they will significantly reduce the density of trees. Rabbits inhibit tree growth when rainfall is high. In wiping out seedlings and juvenile trees less than a yard high, rabbits eliminate shade for livestock, increase sheet erosion and weeds, decrease landscape stability, disrupt nutrient cycling, threaten rare acacia species, and may even decrease genetic diversity.

A little over a year after my first visit to Owen Springs station with Graham Pearce, I join him one night for a return visit to systematically count rabbits. Using spotlights, we scan both sides of five one-kilometer transect lines. Together we count a total of twelve rabbits. Graham is baffled. Given the rains of the previous year and what CSIRO scientists think they know about rabbit population dynamics, we should have come up with ten times the number we did.

No one in central Australia really knows what to make of this new mystery. But then no one seems willing to take a bet that within six months or a year rabbits won't be found on Owen Springs and similar stations in plague numbers.

RETURNING
TO THE LAND

Pope John Paul II's six-and-a-half-day messianic whirlwind in Australia in August of 1987 was to be highlighted by a half-day stop at Alice Springs. It was universally agreed in the Australian dailies that his visit to the Centre could well prove to be the most memorable part of his journey. The Centre was seen as both geographically and socially symbolic. Moreover, the Pope would be speaking to and with the nation's Aborigines. He would be addressing their problems, not those of other Australians.

In the months preceding the Pope's visit, the twice-weekly local newspaper, *The Centralian Advocate*, was preoccupied with two issues. First, in the interest of the image of the larger community, presumably including Aborigines, could local entrepreneurs be persuaded to cease the sale of alcohol during and immediately preceding the Pope's visit? Few long-term residents in Alice believed that Aborigines would temporarily curb their alcoholic consumption just because the Pope was paying them a special visit. In fact, quite the contrary: Aborigines might, it was feared, see the Pope's visit as a splendid opportunity to drink and brawl in ways heretofore not seen.

The second preoccupation of local journalists was whether non-Aborigines in the community would have equal access to the Pope? Weren't they, after all, also God's children? What was so special about Aborigines, anyway?

An issue of less concern, certainly to the white community, was one raised by the Central Land Council, the principal Aboriginal mouthpiece for Aborigines in the Centre and the organization that would deal directly with the Pope. The leader of the Central Land Council, Pat Dodson, Australia's first Aboriginal Catholic priest (he is no longer a member of the Church, having left after conflicts over his outspoken views on the role of traditional Aboriginal customs within Catholic missions), expressed concern that the Pope would sound like a milksop catering to Australia's white power structure. From Pat Dodson's perspective, the visit would only prove successful if the Pope strongly supported Aboriginal land rights and reaffirmed the need for greater social justice for Aborigines everywhere.

Thousands of Aborigines from all over the Outback came to hear and see and touch the Pope on the afternoon of November 29. No crowd anywhere, I dare say, could have been described as more orderly and respectful. If more than a handful of Aborigines got drunk that day in Alice Springs, I didn't see them. And I was out looking for Aboriginal drunks.

I came and went at will on the fairgrounds where the Pope made his appearance. At the last minute I had no trouble getting within arm's reach of his passing vehicle. No white Australian would have had a problem gaining a similar perspective, had he wanted it.

The Pope's principal message to Aborigines that warm day in The Alice was that they were children of God. He wanted them to know that the message of the Gospel was for them "to become, through and through, Aboriginal Christians. Jesus calls you to accept his words and his values into your own culture. To develop in this way will make you more than ever truly Aboriginal."

Pope John Paul II devoted only a small portion of his speech to Aboriginal land rights. He said that he opposed the legal fiction adopted by European settlers 200 years ago that Australia was *terra nullus*, a land that belonged to nobody and therefore could be claimed under English law. He also reaffirmed "the rights of the Aboriginal inhabitants to traditional lands on which their whole society depended. Let it not be said that fair and equitable recognition of Aboriginal rights to land is discrimination. To call for the acknowledgment of the land rights of people who have never surrendered those rights is not discrimination." But then, in a qualifying remark that must have struck many Aboriginal activists as coming out of the other side of his mouth, he said, "Certainly what has been done cannot be undone. But what can now be done to remedy the deeds of yesterday must not be put off till tomorrow."

The Pope returned to his thoroughly Christianizing message and the words of the Prophets: "I have called you by your name, you are mine."

In 1985 the Trinidadian novelist and nonfiction writer Shiva Naipaul made a visit to the Northern Territory. Eager to get a glimpse of how Aborigines live in the bush, he sought permission to enter Arnhem Land. Before applying for permission, however, Naipaul had dinner with anthropologists and others associated with the Northern Land Council in Darwin, the principal group in charge of Aboriginal affairs. During the course of the evening he referred to Aborigines as "primitives." He went on to say that Aborigines could not be considered to have created a culture as sophisticated as that of the Chinese or the Greeks, the Indians or the Egyptians. As Naipaul tells it, this candor was enough to ensure that he would not be issued a pass for entry into Aboriginal lands anywhere in the Territory.

Not to be deterred by the refusal (his first ever in all of his many peregrinations around the globe, he said), Naipaul subsequently attended a celebration of National Aborigines Week in Darwin. There he allowed his imagination to run free about what he saw, particularly about motives and states of mind he could infer from dress, body movements, prejudices embedded in his own history. Based on these few experiences—dinner and attendance at a celebration, his reading of newspaper articles and of Anthony Trollope's account of his visit to Australia in 1872— and on Naipaul's own knowledge of Third World movements, Naipaul concluded that the Land Rights Act of 1976, which for the first time returned land to Aborigines in the Territory, had simply become an occasion for a "flight into blackness."

Naipaul argued that the government's attempt at restitution and its fervid execution by acculturated mixed-blood Aborigines

is a fad that has all the "familiar lineaments of so-called liberation struggles the world over." He said that to believe that the
Aborigines can be anything other than a petitioner at the gates
of white Australia is a delusion, one certain to result in political
disaster.

It is one thing to reinterpret and rewrite the Aboriginal past,
to reach a new understanding of the virtues (and vices) of a
society so long ignored and denigrated. No harm is done if
the settler kingdom should experience tremors of anxiety
and see its own past in a different, less heroic light. Self
knowledge may be alarming, but without it we remain in a
state of arrested development, prey to spurious vanities not
worth the cost of the ink and the stone used to celebrate
them. But it is quite another thing, in the name of restitution, to deform our vision of the present and its needs, to
invoke afresh cultures and identities ravaged by time and
contact and powerlessness. These attempted acts of restora-
tion are not merely dishonest; they are cruel. Too much has
happened.

Not long after Naipaul's ruminations on the Aboriginal movement were published in *The Sydney Morning Herald,* Pat Dodson, by then director of the Central Land Council in Alice
Springs, responded to Naipaul. Dodson's position was that although Aborigines are, admittedly, a hyphenated culture living
astride two worlds, they have adapted to the new order only
reluctantly and they owe primary allegiance to Aboriginal tradition and law. "We live in houses, we use telephones, we have
electricity," Dodson said, "but we also cook kangaroo in the
backyard and eat most of the bush food."

He then added: "It is almost impossible for Aboriginal people
to participate continually in Western society and hope to carry
out the obligations they have under our law."

Despite the massive and irreversible changes wrought on Aboriginal people, Dodson said that "non-Aboriginal people [are] a
mere hiccup in the history of our people's occupation of this
land." Anxious to emphasize that Aboriginal customs—or what
remain of them—must persist, he concluded that "if Aboriginal

people one day said that they wanted to be assimilated into a non-Aboriginal society, then they would definitely be lost." Pat Dodson believed that by allowing his people to return to land that was once theirs everything would somehow succeed. In his view, Aboriginal time and Aboriginal traditions are timeless.

Within four years of passage of the Northern Territory Land Rights Act of 1976, Aborigines owned twenty-eight percent of the Territory. They had lodged claims for another eighteen percent. At this time, Aboriginal land ownership elsewhere in the six Australian states ranged from a high of eleven percent in South Australia to lows of 206 square kilometers in New South Wales and one square kilometer in Tasmania, or one five-hundredth of one percent of that island state. Even in South Australia, which arguably had initiated land rights in Australia in 1966, Aborigines possessed only long-term leases, not the freehold title they held in the Northern Territory.

These gains by Aborigines contrast favorably to those of Canadian Indians, who, though long in possession of land, have always had less than full property rights and have rarely been in an enviable position when bargaining with their government for redress of injustices. Nor has the case been much different for native Americans in the United States. When native Alaskans came to a settlement over land rights with the U.S. government in 1971, they didn't fare nearly so well as did the Territory's Aborigines.

Land, of course, is not of equal value, either to nomadic hunters and gatherers, who may treasure it as much for its religious significance as for its economic resources, or to those in modern societies trading in industrial and agricultural products. Most of the land given to Aborigines in the Northern Territory had been established as reserves and missions in the nineteenth century; it was land thought worthless, or too remote, or inhospitable—perfect for keeping "blackfellas" out of the white man's way. More than half of the Territory's land that passed to Aborigines after 1976 is harsh desert or semi-desert, considered at best marginal for cattle or other livestock. Of the remainder, a significant portion has proved to be rich in minerals (uranium, bauxite, gold), an issue that now threatens the very existence of the Land Rights Act since, unlike other Australians, Aborigines have effective control of resources beneath the ground. A small fraction of the land owned by the Territory's Aborigines—less than ten percent—is pastoral property once held by whites. Purchased for Aborigines with government grants and loans, virtually all of the cattle stations—more than a dozen in all—were bought under two guises: that they were important traditional lands to which Aboriginal people wanted to return, and that the stations would be operated as viable economic units just as they had been by white Australians. Today the Aboriginal land councils and development commissions of the Northern Territory continue to try to buy cattle stations. They insist that they can be run for profit, much as they always have been.

The Hayes family arrived in the Centre in 1884. They first established Undoolya station, and then nearby Owen Springs and Deep Well stations. The three stations, all within an hour or so of Alice Springs, remain in the Hayes family to this day. At the Doreen Braitling Memorial Lecture in Alice Springs in 1983, Ted Hayes, the octogenarian owner of Undoolya, had this to say about his family's relationship with Aborigines:

> In spite of what you sometimes read and hear about the Aborigines and the early white settlers of that period, there were always good relations. Each required assistance from the other. The blacks of course were the unskilled labour required for general station work under supervision. They learned to appreciate the first aid and limited medical attention that was available from the early pioneer families, and they were very faithful workers, very rarely leaving the properties, only for their occasional walkabout, mostly after the seasonal rains. The Aborigines I am speaking about were the first generation from the tribal blacks, who in one generation had learned to accept the whiteman's food and customs. They were greatly appreciated by the early settlers, and the groups of Aborigines that lived around the stations were people that belonged to that particular area.

The native women were very fond of the white station children, and taught them their skills. Aborigines generally accepted white children born on the stations as members of the tribe.

When European pastoralists first moved into the Northern Territory in the nineteenth century, a special clause in their leases allowed Aborigines to live on the land, use natural water holes, and hunt native animals. In 1924 the provision became territorial law. Since cattlemen could not get by without Aboriginal labor, they neither took much notice of the law nor showed any concern for small Aboriginal settlements on their leases. When, however, in 1968 Aborigines were awarded pay equal to that of whites for station work, pastoralists got rid of most of their Aboriginal stockmen. They decided they could do without the high-priced labor and would, instead, muster their cattle with helicopters. It was time to tell Aborigines who had lived on their leases, many for fifty years or more, to find someplace else to call home.

In 1973 the Woodward Royal Commission on land rights recommended a strengthening of Aboriginal rights on pastoral properties. Justice Woodward recommended that Aborigines be granted living areas on the leases and have free access to well water. These recommendations were ignored in the historic Northern Territory Land Rights Act of 1976. Subsequently, however, a high court decided that stock routes, over which cattlemen had traditionally moved their cattle to market, could be claimed by Aborigines under the Land Rights Act. Although these routes might conceivably be used as community lands, they usually are inferior; they may, for example, be far distant from dream trails and sacred sites that figure prominently in clan rituals. With this in mind, Aboriginal land councils in the Territory informed pastoralists that they would drop claims against the stock routes in exchange for the right to buy small pieces of land on the stations. Aborigines wanted excisions large enough to grow a few crops and maintain small cattle herds.

The proposal has not met with favor. Cattlemen have strongly opposed the whole idea of land rights from the beginning, and they refused to accept the fact that Aborigines could now claim stock routes under the Land Rights Act. As with their leases, so with the government-owned and maintained routes along which they had once run their cattle: through long use, they felt they preemptively owned the rights-of-way. Nor has the Northern Territory government been an ally of the Aborigine on the excision issue. For an Aborigine to qualify under Territory guidelines, he must have been a resident on the property for the previous ten years and he must show that he has not rented a house elsewhere during that time.

Despite the huge size of stations in the Centre, virtually all of them including sizeable patches of worthless spinifex or feed-poor land, only a handful of pastoralists have been willing to sell a tiny piece of their leaseholds to Aborigines. From 1973 to 1983, eleven cattlemen in the whole of the Territory were so generous.

The impending sale of Ammaroo station had received a prominent place in the Alice Springs newspaper a good two months in advance of the auction. Advertised as a "renowned cattle-fattening property" containing 3,014 square kilometers, "sensibly improved," with an "excellent plant," a lease that was good until the year 2012 at a yearly rental of $A803.16, and an average turnoff of 1,246 cattle over the previous ten years, it was anyone's guess what the station would fetch in open bidding. In the early 1970s it might have sold for $250,000, by the early 1980s for more than three times that figure. Now the rumor was that it would certainly go for more than a million dollars. A couple of station owners allegedly were prepared to pay as much as 1.3 million.

Was the Aboriginal Development Commission, on behalf of Aborigines, interested in buying the station? No one I talked with on the Commission in the months preceding the auction seemed to know; or they weren't talking. What they would say was that whites didn't want to sell their stations to blacks. Some years ago one of the stations in the Centre had been purchased by a white Queenslander who, to all outward appearances, wanted to invest in the Territory. In fact, he was acting on behalf of the Aboriginal Development Commission. As members of a small community, where gossip flows like beer through a six o'clock tap, proud cattlemen weren't likely to forget this hoodwinking anytime soon.

When I arrived at the Alice Sheraton a half-hour before the bidding was to begin, some forty people were milling about the bar in the hotel lobby. I got myself a drink and, seeing no familiar faces, stood off to one side. The mood was relaxed, as if everyone were enjoying a final gin or scotch after the last running at the racetrack. The men, whom I guessed to be station owners, were dressed casually, in slacks and open-necked short-sleeve shirts. They had good tans and close-cropped hair; several were portly, balding, showing their middle age. The women among them wore tasteful print dresses and simple jewelry. I guessed they were station wives, but they could have easily been town secretaries or real estate agents.

The auction was launched by a youthful lawyer in tie and long-sleeve shirt, who meticulously listed Ammaroo's assets and the conditions for sale. After he finished with a reminder that 300 of the station's cows could be sold as soon as the papers were signed, an Elders Pastoral agent took to the podium, laid out the ground rules, and suggested an opening bid of one million dollars. Getting no takers, he promptly dropped the opening price to three-quarters of a million. A fat showy man in the front row lurched forward and bellowed a joke that no one seemed to understand, then raised his hand for a first bid. Three others soon joined in.

The bidding rose quickly in increments of $25,000. Somewhere just above the million mark it became a two-party show. Neither of the bidders had the appearance of pastoralists I'd met or had begun to fix in my mind's eye. One sat slouched about midway along the main aisle with an ungainly leg propped ankle on knee. Wearing aqua shorts, a worn football jersey, and tennis shoes, he appeared to be no more than thirty. Soon it would become apparent that he was representing someone else, a white-haired, rosy-cheeked man directly across the aisle, who was a well-known pastoralist with a station adjacent to Ammaroo. The other bidder appeared equally out of character. Leaning casually against a side wall, his arms folded, he had an unkempt salt-and-pepper beard, a good crop of hair, and was wearing thick black-rimmed glasses. He could easily have been taken for a high school teacher satisfying a curiosity.

The bidding between the two moved quickly along until it approached 1.4 million. Then it dropped to increments of ten thousand, and then five thousand after it passed 1.6 million. Above 1.5 million, the bearded bidder began to shift around on the wall and wait for the last moment before popping a splayed hand into view. By this time, the guy in shorts, who, it turned out, was an accountant, had straightened up in his chair and now waited for the nodding okay from across the aisle before raising the price. Just short of 1.7 million dollars, the bearded one asked if he could increase the bid by $500. The crowd giggled, as if he'd meant it as a joke. The request was made to look ridiculous by the suave Elders' agent. But it soon became apparent that the bearded bidder wasn't kidding; he had reached his limit and could not better the previous bid. The war of numbers now over, the agent opened the envelope containing the seller's minimum acceptable offer. He announced that the high bid had been too low. He consulted with the seller and then said that negotiations between the high bidder and the seller would take place in private.

As the crowd began to disperse, I cornered the bearded bidder. "The price seemed high," I said. "I wouldn't have thought that with even a great turn-off rate and a small mortgage there'd be any hope of making a decent return on investment."

"You pay whatever it's worth to you. Put enough into it, you'll get your money back."

"You mean the new buyer will have to flog the hell out of the land, practically kill it."

He smiled at the corners of his mouth.

"You're a station owner, I gather?"

"No."

"You've run a station then?"

"Have worked on some. I know what I need to." He turned away, began to leave.

I stayed with him and asked, "Have you been in the Territory long?"

"Eight years," he said, and then ran off.

I'd wanted to ask if he was there to buy the station for Aborigines.

More than three hours north of Alice Springs, over half this time on dirt and gravel track, lies the Aboriginal land known as Utopia. Originally purchased as a cattle station and at one time well stocked, it now lacks even a small "kill herd" for the local needs of its 400-plus black residents. Today its only business is the production of batiks by women for tourists. The station's men spend their days hunting with low-caliber rifles for scarce kangaroos, emu, and bush turkeys. They also tinker with their battered secondhand cars and dying Toyota trucks, eagerly waiting for another dole check so they can gamble, buy grog, and get enough petrol to pay a visit to neighboring kinsmen.

Utopia failed as a cattle station because it had not a single Aboriginal leader with enough power to bring its several competing groups together in pursuit of a common objective. Aborigines find it difficult to work with an authority structure larger than the local clan. Still enmeshed in the web of tradition, they like to live apart in small, discontinuous, largely self-sufficient groups, on what are known as outstations. While the development of ten outstations at Utopia allowed kin groups to pursue their religious and personal interests, it also laid the foundation for disharmony, misunderstanding, and failure in the livestock business. There were continual battles over who should fix the fences, who should take care of the wells and bores, who should brand cattle and move them among paddocks, whose cattle were mustered and who, therefore, was entitled to the proceeds of a sale. Compounding these troubles, the elders complained because some had vehicles and others didn't. In the new Aboriginal society of the late twentieth century, vehicle ownership is one clear measure of prestige. As soon as Utopia was granted freehold title in 1984 and was, therefore, no longer subject to government covenants, the elders sold the last of the station's diminishing herd of cattle and purchased expensive Toyota trucks.

I'd first heard about Stumpy Martin's untimely death while having a beer in the Tea-Tree roadhouse. Until he died, Stumpy Martin had been the Aboriginal leader on Willowra, a large cattle station two-and-a-half hours by difficult dirt track northwest of Tea-Tree. In good mourning tradition, Stumpy Martin's relations would be leaving their homes for a month or more. The search would soon begin for another leader. As for Stumpy Martin, his name would never again be spoken by those Aborigines in Willowra and elsewhere who heeded the traditional taboo against voicing the name of a deceased kinsman.

But among whites around Tea-Tree and others far to the north and south, Stumpy's name would not soon be forgotten. As a former employee of the Aboriginal Development Corporation, as one reputed to be equally at ease among whites and traditional Aborigines, Stumpy led an unusual life. From time to time he could be seen strutting about The Alice in the latest finery, or betting large sums of money on craps and roulette at the casino. There Stumpy would lose as much as five thousand dollars in a single night. He was, I heard over the course of several months, a man of other excesses as well. He loved new cars and Toyota trucks, and he had a fondness for showering money and expensive gifts on close kin. Stumpy Martin, it was no secret, had secured his short-lived wealth by absconding with the assets of his Walpiri kinsmen, all of whom are co-owners in trust of the cattle station at Willowra.

Initially settled by whites in the 1920s, Willowra had a checkered history until the early 1940s. It changed hands several times, cattle numbers fluctuated wildly, and few improvements were made. Then, during the drought years of the 1960s, the cattle population of the 4,900-square-kilometer station dropped below 1,500. It then rebounded after several successive years of good rains. By 1979, and now under Aboriginal control, 10,000 head of cattle were grazing the land.

Exactly what went wrong with Willowra's effort to run a profitable cattle station remains a bit of a mystery. Aboriginal Development Corporation employees in Alice Springs will not talk about the station's failure, except in vague generalities. Since those at the ADC are responsible for the procuring and accounting of funds from the federal government and have given Willowra sizeable sums over the years for fencing and herd improvement, they understandably are embarrassed by Stumpy Martin's profligate behavior and the failure of what was once a showcase for similar Aboriginal efforts in the Territory.

In broad outline, the explanation for the cattle station's demise includes the following: poor management and a half-hearted interest in the cattle business; inattention to the government's program to rid the station of brucellosis and tuberculosis; and the continual drain on resources by Stumpy Martin. In the early 1980s most of the station's remaining livestock was sold. The handsome proceeds allowed Stumpy Martin several extravagant flings before he died of a heart attack.

When Tea-Tree station was bought for Aborigines in 1976 with the explicit purpose of making it a viable cattle operation, it was in bad shape. Fences were broken, wells and bores needed repair, and tuberculosis was a large-scale problem. Rather than attempt to muster the cattle and clean it up through testing and culling, it was thought more economical to destock the entire station. This happened in 1979. Thereafter the ADC moved slowly to find someone to undertake necessary repairs and restock and manage Tea-Tree. The ADC had no Aboriginal candidates, nor did it see a way of giving one on-the-job training under the tutelage of an experienced white manager. In 1984, however, it hired Craig Steen, an American who had grown up on a cattle and sheep station in South Australia, to run the station's store. Because of their considerable isolation, station owners with large Aboriginal populations have long been in the practice of operating stores stocked with dry goods and a minimal supply of meat and fruit and vegetables.

Not long after Craig and his family arrived at Tea-Tree, Craig was asked by the ADC to become the station's manager. It was stipulated that until the station became profitable, Craig would be guaranteed a salary by the ADC. His wife, Sylvie, could take over management of the store, for which she would receive an income from the profits. In addition, Craig and Sylvie would be paid for distributing the fortnightly dole checks to the resident Aborigines.

With virtually no hands-on experience in the cattle business, Craig set about mending fences, repairing wells, fixing trucks and other equipment, and mustering feral horses to be sold to the abattoir. He sold a lot of brumbies, all that he could find. But progress has been slow, and at the time I talked with Craig there were a mere 300 cows on the station. Craig had no idea what the number would be in one, two, or five years, or even whether the station would ever again carry 5,000 head of cattle, as it once had. And should the station be revitalized, there's the problem of finding or training an Aboriginal head stockman. He employs one, but he comes from a clan that lives on an adjoining station to the south. Craig uses half a dozen local Aborigines for about two to four weeks a year. They do a little fence work and push cattle to ungrazed paddocks. Since they are on the dole, Craig pays them in food from the store.

Because of the very considerable capital now required to buy a cattle station in the Centre, Craig and Sylvie Steen have given up on their dream of ever owning one. Among the few certainties for the Steens is that in seven or eight years, when their children are too old for the school in Tea-Tree, they plan to return to the United States. For the moment they're happy with their income. They love the Centre, and they enjoy working with Aborigines.

"What are some of the problems you've had since coming to the station?" I asked.

One of the hardest things for me," Sylvie said, "was getting used to all the dirt and filth." She explained that their two children had strong friendships with several of the Aboriginal children. "If only there weren't so many lice in their hair all the time!"

Then, perhaps thinking I'd form a mistaken impression about Aborigines, Sylvie noted that while they had broken the windows in most of their government homes and preferred to sleep under the stars and cook over open fires and wash their clothes in the creek, they had their own sense of cleanliness. When the Steens asked them why didn't they live in the houses built for them, they said it was because they "couldn't stand the smells."

Craig, who describes himself as part stockman, part counselor, part mechanic, and part handyman, says that in the beginning they had no time to themselves. There was hardly an hour of the day or night when there wasn't a knock at their door for a favor: to listen to a domestic problem or intercede in a fight, to borrow a piece of equipment, to ask for money. Finally, they established rules and hours during which they would be available. Now Craig's principal problems are fending off demands to use the station's truck and teaching Aboriginal residents to treat it with respect: "So they don't just bang it all up going cross-country over any old track while chasing a 'roo or bowling through a fence because it's a short cut."

Near the end of our conversation, I asked Craig, "Are you training anyone to take over management of the station?"

He repeated that he'd hired an Aboriginal stockman from a nearby station. Then he came to a full stop. His face took on a quizzical look, as if I'd asked a question whose answer I should've been able to deduce from all that we'd just talked about.

There are no more than two or three economically successful Aboriginal cattle stations in the whole of the Northern Territory, and all of them are managed by whites. They are run by men who have successfully managed other cattle stations or by previous owners retained as expensive managers or consultants under Aboriginal ownership.

One obvious reason for the station failings is that virtually no serious effort has been made to train Aborigines in station management. It is one thing to be able to muster and brand cattle and move them among paddocks; it is quite another to know how to set up a rational system of paddock use, to determine optimal turn-off rates, and to be able to identify good markets. Yet even with rigorous training programs in station management, and making the dubious assumption that Aborigines would have open access to "white" markets for their cattle, it is doubtful that many of the stations could economically succeed in the way they once did. One reason is that Aborigines in the Centre have a poorly developed sense of saving and capital investment, which is quite understandable given a tradition bereft of the concepts of money and accumulation. Another problem is that a younger generation of Aborigines does not share its elders' strong historical and emotional attachment to cattle station life. It is the elders who have argued longest and hardest that they wanted to do the only thing they had ever known: get on a horse and muster cattle. Furthermore, on many of the stations, as on Utopia, there are seemingly insoluble differences among Aboriginal groups. Because the boundaries of contemporary cattle stations bear no relationship to the dream trail and sacred site geography of particular tribal or linguistic groups, several groups often legitimately claim custodial rights to a single station.

As if these reasons weren't enough for the failure of Aboriginal cattle stations, it is also true that most of them occupy the Centre's poorer grazing lands, which are too dry or have too much useless spinifex or have been flogged to death by previous white owners. When a good station comes up for sale, one with a healthy landbase and well-maintained plant, investors or knowledgeable white cattlemen jump to pay the going market price. When even an average station is put on the market it may be bought by a neighboring station owner to complement his own holdings (as with Ammaroo) or simply to keep it out of Aboriginal hands. Aboriginal representatives can do virtually nothing to combat this racism. They can bid only ten percent above an amount previously determined in protracted negotiation with the government, a fact not lost on white cattlemen bidding at auction.

The average profitable cattle station in the Centre has never employed more than half a dozen people on a full-time basis. By the late 1970s, some ninety plus cattle stations in the Alice

Springs District were providing employment for 264 people; of these, only 46 were working specifically as stockmen. The number of employable men on Aboriginal cattle stations is presently between ten and twenty times this number. Moreover, population growth on these stations currently is quite high, both because of a very high birth rate and because of significant immigration from surrounding stations that remain in white hands. Thus, even if one imagines the rosiest of economic scenarios for Aboriginal cattle stations, the profits are not nearly enough to give all individuals resident on them anything approaching a decent standard of living.

It is gratuitous and shortsighted to argue that Aborigines are content to hunt and forage for bush tucker and to live with a lower standard of living than that aspired to by most white Australians. Aborigines may indeed be content with little, by white standards, for the near future, but as their large and growing young population loses its sense of the traditional past and is forced more and more into mainstream Australian society, it will surely seek a lifestyle closer to the national norm.

There is another complication. With the exception of the manager and perhaps the head stockman on these stations, it would be hard to find more than a handful of Aborigines not on the dole. Not only are there few jobs, there are no incentives for them to take those that occasionally become available. An Aborigine with four children receives more in dole money than he would by working a standard forty-four hour week as a station hand under the award wage.

Nor are Aborigines blind to simple social and economic calculations. If one is on the dole, why bother to muster or mend fences? Receiving money for work in addition to the dole is illegal. Besides, given Aboriginal social structure, working for this extra income yields little return because there persists a strong tradition of sharing whatever one has with all manner of kin. Only a few Aborigines, keen to their own needs and with an incipient sense of saving, ask white station managers to put aside part of their dole money so they don't have to pass it around to every outstretched hand.

The present economic cost to the government of keeping station Aborigines on the dole is minimal. But surely as these populations grow—and they are among the fastest growing groups in Australia—the bill will rise sharply. Of greater concern is the human cost, the fact that remoteness alone insures that none of these Aborigines has access to meaningful job training. They are ignorant and uneducated now and they will remain so as long as they are encouraged to live in small outstation clusters far from towns.

Some Aboriginal leaders, like Pat Dodson, and some whites, most of whom are city-bred liberals in search of a cause, are quick to point out that the purchase and settlement of Aboriginal stations is part of the policy of self-determination, that Aborigines are consciously deciding to return to the land and they know what they are doing. They speak of a "profound attachment to ancestral lands, an attachment which upholds strong and coherent social structures." The tenor of these arguments sings with a timelessness, as if little has changed and even less is likely to change in the future. If only Aborigines are left to their own ways, beyond the sphere of ethnocentric judgments, they will remain ever happy. The case thus put is a strong and undiluted version of Australia's policy of multiculturalism, that of letting people of different traditions be what they will and do what they will.

A heady and liberating principle this multiculturalism, and one perhaps easily supported if one is talking about bilingualism, the maintenance of strong family values, education to foster appreciation of cultural traditions. But for a people with one foot firmly lodged in a cultural system utterly out of sync with a larger society certain to dominate and control every aspect of the future, guidance is required. The Aborigine of today is not the Aborigine of yesterday, nor is he the Aborigine of tomorrow. He cannot hide; in changing as much as he has, he has made that impossible.

What is wrong with Aboriginal cattle stations is not really that they don't work as European-style economic units. Indeed, given the awful condition of so much of the Centre's pastoral lands, an ecologically minded sort might sensibly argue for the continuing purchase of cattle stations for Aborigines, all the while entertaining the hope that all of them will fail. No, what is fundamentally wrong with them is that they encourage the formation of distant rural slums, places remote, out of sight, and easily forgotten. Their creation only postpones the day of responsible reckoning by white and Aboriginal leaders alike.

REASONING
WITH THE HEART

We move into a two-room cement-block house on what was once a poultry farm. Before the owner had a heart attack and had to call it quits, he raised and slaughtered chickens. At any one time he had up to 20,000 birds on hand. Now only eight are left—just enough to lay several eggs a day, to eat the raw garbage tossed out the back door, and to serve as a dependable alarm clock, if you like getting up at first light.

These few survivors now wander the former farm as if they've been here forever. As soon as we let them out of their coop in the morning they begin patrolling among the wiry buckbush and pigweed, circling beneath the tangled corkwoods, the dying prickly wattle interlaced with flowering mistletoe, the dead ghost gum out back that was ringbarked by pigs.

One morning I watch the chickens with newfound curiosity as I sip coffee. I follow three of them as they strut and swing down the dirt road toward the chained gate and the portentous KEEP OUT sign that warns of contagious diseases. The clucking trio gets lost within the shadows of a half-constructed two-story mansion, and I find myself wondering what they're looking for. I'm not always able to remember that only humans have motives.

I return to my senses, wonder why I'm contemplating an animal that figures so prominently in my diet when there's so much other amazing company around us.

Take, for example, the sleek gecko that scooted up the yellow wall before disappearing behind the spice rack early this morning. I was in a trance for long minutes as I waited for it to reappear. Now I'll look for it every morning, try to guess whether I'm seeing the same one or another member of an elusive family. Maybe every morning I'll have the same thought: Come around tonight about ten or eleven and feast on the insects that gather at my bedside lamp. What a meal you'll have!

Or take, for example, the creamy freckled frogs that I sometimes find in the bathroom sink upon rising. At night, usually about eight o'clock, they come out of nowhere to spend an hour or two on the inside edges of the high windows. They startle me with the shrill screech of tortured madmen trapped within the resonating bowels of the toilet.

Then there's that furry tan spider the size of a silver dollar that hasn't moved from its spot above the front door for two days now. Upon waking I wonder what task, what complex spidery thought, could possibly take so long. Out of ignorance I suppose, I assume the spider, because of its color, is harmless. I don't even see a need to banish it from the house.

Yesterday afternoon, as I strolled out back, a screeching red-tailed black cockatoo descended from the northern sky to claim a perch on the dead ghost gum. Within minutes he was joined by a score of others. Speaking nonstop in some unknowable tongue, all of them took turns flitting and hopping among the high branches, then singly and in pairs they glided down to boards and branches near the horses' iron water trough before claiming drinking perches. Back and forth between tree and trough the huge cackling cockatoos flew, their black and scarlet tails splayed, showing off magnificently—just for me, I half imagined.

Aboriginal legend has it that when white men came into this country they killed the red-tailed black cockatoos to steal the fire carried in their flaming tails.

East of here a couple of miles I know the whereabouts of an even larger flock of red-tails. There were thirty-nine the last time I was there. They came howling in raucous waves to claim two gorgeous ironwoods. Seven of them, all with their black crowns raised like Chinese fans, perched on the very highest branches. Two of this lot had faded yellow beaks and chalky yellowish stippling that ran through their breast feathers like garlic powder sprinkled on a black rug. The others had slate-gray beaks; their breast feathers were indistinguishable from the blackness elsewhere on their imposing forms. A light-beaked cockatoo and a dark-beaked one snuggled up to one another, forming what seemed to be a perfect pair.

There are days when I would describe these red-tails as creatures of habit, neatly attuned to the solar clock. One day they come at 5:10, a couple of days later at 5:11, then at 5:12. Then, upsetting the facile generality I'm about to claim on their behalf, they don't come at all for several days. Did they find a more attractive water site? Did some large social event along the Todd or Charles river interrupt their normal schedule? Or do they simply make the rounds of six, eight, a dozen watering sites here and elsewhere in the MacDonnell Ranges?

Nor do I understand other habits. One day last week they stayed atop those ironwoods for a mere twenty-one minutes; then something startled them. Or rather, it first startled the five crested pigeons that had been relegated to the lower limbs when the cockatoos arrived. What frightened them enough to put them on the wing? Not I, surely; I was motionless, a silent prisoner to their every twitch. I saw nothing on the ground, nothing around the base of the trees, beyond. But then my senses are poorly attuned to some of nature's sounds, certain of its warnings, what goes on in the minds of birds.

Aborigines have thought that birds, if not exactly intelligent, at least possess special powers. When European explorers first came upon the Aborigines of the Centre, girls and young women were not permitted to eat the flesh of bush turkeys and wedge-tailed eagles until their breasts were fully developed. Should an Aboriginal woman do so, it was believed that her breasts would stop growing. When women were asked why their breasts were so small, they would explain that it was because they'd eaten forbidden meat when they were young. These beliefs, these rules, it might be surmised, were made less to cater to a male interest in large breasts than out of a concern with the greater nurturing possibilities suggested by breast size. Aboriginal women kept children on the breast for the first three years of life.

The prohibition against eating certain birds and animals took a somewhat different form for young males. Until they reached manhood, they were allowed to eat only the legs of wedge-tailed eagles. The meager flesh on the legs was thought to impart strength, to improve the growth of limbs.

A cage on one side of our temporary home is full of chattering budgies. A cage on the other side holds only two, a plump green and blue pair trying to make babies. In an enclosure fashioned from a homemade camper top, which lies on the ground next to a field of galloping pigweed and squash yellow bush buttons, is a pair of rambunctious galahs. They spend their days pasted to their prison door, bathing in real light, envious, it seems, of brethren flying by. When I approach them they retreat to a far corner, there to huddle in fright in the darkness.

The first afternoon we're here I change their water and feed the birds sunflower seeds. I sit on my haunches for several long minutes watching them, and then I realize that I have a strong urge to leave the cage door open and walk away. One morning I catch sight of one of the captive galahs waving its head from side to side. I wonder if the bird is going mad in its desire for freedom. I consider a slightly more mischievous thought: leave the door open and then bang the far side of the cage to force them out. Reclaim the sky, you two!

Early one evening I hear a prolonged staccato cry. I run to the door and see a strange fluttering motion on the high branch of a ghost gum; I reach for binoculars. A galah, a juvenile with pale pink feathers, is sitting on a denuded branch below one of its parents. Shoulders extended, head back and beak open, the young one is crying for food. The parent obliges by dipping its beak into the open mouth, then regurgitating mushy seed from its ample crop. The dependant youth takes in all it can, straightens up to swallow, then repeats the piercing call. Again and again the ritual is enacted, until the offspring is sated.

Sometimes while walking along a road or through a field I come upon fifty, seventy-five, a hundred galahs feeding on the ground. Mere inches from one another, they all face and feed in the same direction, so that with the slightest hint of danger the entire flock can take to the air without the worry of a collision. When a new bird joins the feeding flock it instinctively turns and faces in the right direction. Those in the rear, who search ground already picked over, tolerate their second-class status only so long; then, as if cued by an alarm on a timer, they fly to the front of the flock to get their turn at fresh ground. How orderly, symmetrical, rational, marvelously egalitarian!

Several months ago I read in the local Alice Springs newspaper that the secretary of the Central Australian Football League wanted to eliminate galahs from the town's Traeger Park Oval because the birds were eating the grass and scarring the playing surface. They had been attracted to the park because of the luscious greenery; this part of the Centre had had almost no rainfall for more than a year and the galahs were pressed for feed. Now the secretary was concerned because the birds were making the playing surface "uneven and unsightly and posing danger to the football players." A player could twist his ankle. "We're trying to develop the best oval in Australia," the secretary said, dismissing the "fourth-generation galahs because they look upon the place as a sanctuary." Which, I suppose, was a roundabout way of saying that enough of the pink pests had had their day in the sun on the footy grass and it was time for them to go. The secretary had convinced a city commissioner to use an "aerial scarecrow" imported from the south, an artificial bird that looked like a small kite. It would hover at the end of a long wire and be pushed about by the wind. If the galahs weren't scared off, then, the secretary insisted, the birds would have to be eliminated. I sensed that the least of his concerns was the Northern Territory law that defined galahs as a protected species.

I can't seem to fathom why Kevin and Angela, lovers of animals and caretakers of this property until it finds another buyer with a new idea, imprison these birds. Why would anyone, since the gum trees and acacias all around us are full of galahs? Are there good reasons for caging winged creatures?

Most Outback Australians despise galahs, consider them bothersome pests. The birds are infamous for destroying crops, tearing up grass on rugby fields, stripping trees of their leaves and so killing them, yelling in maddening unison when you want silence. Any of these reasons, Aussies will tell you, is reason enough to use galahs for target practice.

The idea of shooting any galah repels me, and I don't entirely know why. There are millions of them all over Australia. The native/non-native distinction aside, it's not too farfetched to say that galahs are akin to America's sparrows: taken for granted, too commonplace to want to care about, easy scapegoats for exaggerated abuses, considered mere junk life.

I wonder if my attitude has something to do with the size of galahs; they're medium-sized parrots, as big as well-fed crows. Or is it the striking color that seduces me, that soft bridal pink on sunlit grey? Is it the intelligence I've come to attribute to all parrots? Is it the way the galahs size me up and cant their egg-shaped heads and stare at me with those thick loopy eyes when I crook my neck to watch them high above in a coolibah? Is it the frequency with which I see them flying in pairs? Mom and Dad, I often think out loud; then smile to myself, wanting to get on the wing to follow them home, admire their young, feel their warmth in my hands.

I wonder if it's because I mindlessly killed a robin with a BB gun when I was eleven. I couldn't stand myself for weeks after I'd picked up the warm grey-brown and red body and gawked at the head hanging from my hand like a wet noodle.

We might have been given her name by Kevin or Angela before they left, but I don't think so. So we simply call her the nameless one. Black and sleek and gentle, with a gimpy right front leg, she appears only for a brief time in the morning and again at dinner, when we try our darndest to get her to eat something. God, how finicky this cat can be! We try everything in the refrigerator, on our plates, and she barely eats.

Honest to God, the nameless one seems to like little other than minced sirloin steak. Eat nameless one! Are you trying to starve yourself to death? Or are you, wily creature, robbing bird nests, expertly prowling high grass to ambush lizards? Are you a mighty three-legged hunter of the night who sees no reason to come to us but for small treats and that fresh bowl of milk?

At least Sally's not like this. A big lumbering Dalmatian, she's an easy one to please. Cat food, dog food, lamb fat, chicken skin—anything's okay with Sally. Sally has a special predilection for the nameless one's food. Put food out for the cat when Sally's around and she'll disarm you with a wagging smile or stand on her hind legs and lick your cheek, begging. I nod and Sally runs for the plate, gobbles up the food, licks the edge, thanks me, then sniffs around beneath the plate for a morsel she might have missed.

Then there's Cammy, the seven-year-old thoroughbred that Kevin rides all the time. The first day that Kevin is gone Cammy won't leave me alone. He comes to the front door and sticks his nose in, whinnies, nuzzles me back. Cammy wants in; I'm tempted to say, Why not? Kevin probably allows it.

When I go for a stroll to mull over what I've written, Cammy follows. If I pretend to ignore him, he nudges me, brushes me on the back, nips at a pant leg. He wants me to stop and rub his face, scratch him, brush his forelocks. He misses Kevin.

I don't see all that much of Cammy during the day. I know he's out there somewhere. I hear his voice, pick up the boom and roar of an unprovoked playful gallop. Now and again I look out the front door and see Cammy tearing away at the grass out front; no lawn mower necessary here. Sometimes I see him strolling through a distant paddock, perhaps to join up with six other horses kept by Kevin and Angela. Or, if I go for a short walk, I just might see Cammy by the old slaughterhouse, and then I'm forced to imagine him listening to Australian folk music and call-in talk shows that wash across the farm from a radio sitting on the slaughterhouse windowsill. Cammy likes the company, he understands what he hears; Kevin told us so before he left. "So I hope you don't mind if the radio's on all the time," Kevin said. All the time: twenty-four hours a day, Kevin implied.

Well, for all I know, it might well be that Cammy really does get off on all this Australian bush lyric and antipodean psychobabble. But it's probably closer to the mark to say that Kevin and Angela have their minds absolutely stuck on horses. In the one small room in which we live (the other one's a toilet, a shower, a laundry room and half-kitchen), I count no less than nine framed photographs of horses on the walls. Plus three calendars, all of them horse calendars. Plus nearly fifty blue and red and yellow and white and green three-foot by two-inch ribbons that serve as curtains or hang like party decorations from the walls. Plus—on a small freezer, on a speaker, on top of the TV, on top of the refrigerator, on top of a knick-knack table, on the floor itself because there's not enough room—more than twenty trophies won in horse competitions, trophies for barrel racing, flag racing, American bending, show jumping, sack racing, maiden show jumping. . . .

I like to know how others live, what they like, and nothing brings out the brash snoop in me faster than the sight of books. On a shelf I come upon fifty or sixty paperbacks carelessly stacked to one side of a pile of clothes. Three or four celebrate Elvis, a couple can be called literature, a dozen or more have titles like *A Pony for Tony* or *The Island Stallion*. More than twenty of the books are Dick Francis novels. I've never read a Dick Francis novel, never had any interest in him, but something tells me I'm looking at just about everything written by the jockey-turned-novelist.

The other morning, as I got out of bed to take a pee, I was stabbed in the eye by the early morning light beaming off a dozen of the trophies. Jesus, I thought, what would Kevin and Angela think of me if they knew that just a couple of days before we moved into their house—promising we'd take good care of Cammy and all the other breathing creatures on the property for three weeks—I'd written an article for *The Australian* advocating that the Conservation Commission of the Northern Territory shoot feral horses as soon as they could find enough money and bullets and shooters to do so?

How could I possibly convince Kevin and Angela that I, too, like horses, but that I love irreplaceable things in nature—soils, plants, native wildlife—even more? How should I respond if they claim that horses must always come first after humans on a who-gets-to-live list? What would I say in my defense if they accuse me of being a bloody, cold-hearted Yank bastard for even thinking about shooting horses?

Daily, just before dinner, I open one of the large cans of dog food from the case Kevin and Angela left. I feed Sally her mixture of five meats, horsemeat included.

The sun of the Centre will burn you raw at midday; it bleaches colors and pushes life large and small into hiding. So it's in the late afternoon when I leave the farm and head cross-country for the nearby mountain range to the south. There I can absorb the subtle mint green shades of spinifex, the many-colored reds of the rocky slopes, search for the squat euro that's come out of hiding to eat and drink at its favorite water hole.

I walk this way and that way, and everywhere I see ants running up trees, trail-blazing around or beneath shrubs, busying themselves before scurrying down holes or Grand Canyon crevices. Who, after even a brief stay in the Centre, isn't struck by ant populations that dwarf those in North America?

Some of the early explorers in the Centre thought that only flies were more troublesome than ants. They were so bothered by ants that at times they could not sleep. They would spend their nights walking from one rock outcrop to another, resting for a short while, then moving on to another to avoid them.

In the journals of the famous explorer Ernest Giles there is this description:

> The ants are as rampant as ever, and I passed the night
> in walking up and down the glen. In the morning all the
> horses's legs were puffed and swelled, and they were
> frightened to move from the water. I had great trouble
> getting them down at all. It was impossible to ride them
> away, and here we had to remain for another day, in this
> Inferno. Dante certainly was good at imagining horrors. But
> imagination can't conceive the horror of a region swarming
> with ants; and then Dante never lived in an ant country, and
> had no conception of what torture such creatures can inflict.

The smaller they are the more terrible. My only consolation here was my marble bath, which the horses had polluted; within its cool and shady depths I could alone find respite from my tormenters. Oh, how earnestly did I wish that its waters were the waters of oblivion. . . .

Ants are particularly troublesome around ironwood trees, which travelers and the unwary often seek out for their welcome shade. The notorious small black *Camponotus* concentrates on ironwoods; it loves the night and living flesh. When in country where *Camponotus* was common, early explorers even felt it unsafe to kneel a camel down to adjust its load.

Australia has one of the richest ant faunas in the world, and in a dry creek bed it is possible to find more than a hundred of the two hundred or so species found on the continent. If you sleep in a creek bed you're likely to find yourself being visited by what are known as piss ants, so named because of the urine smell they exude when you squash them. The most famous of the lot, however, are the honeypot ants. Aborigines relish their large repletes, or honey-filled sacks. They search for the small surface openings in the vast cavernous homes in mulga country, then with their digging sticks burrow holes a foot or two deep in search of them. When the ants are found, Aborigines hold them by their heads and with their teeth pop the honey sacks into their mouths. The effort of digging them up doesn't seem anywhere near commensurate with the treat. But then this is a thoroughly Western judgment, one ignorant of both culture and an environment that is largely bereft of sweet edible substances.

One of the Centre's experts on ants told me a story about a distinguished American female scientist who came to Australia several years ago to study the ubiquitous little creatures. After she'd been in the Centre for several weeks, during which she had laid her eyes on mobs and mobs of ants scurrying about in numbers she'd never seen in the deserts of North America, she told the Aussie that something must be wrong. Was this an unusual season? Are we looking at areas disturbed by humans? *What's* wrong? She was visibly disturbed. Something had to be wrong; Australia, she believed, couldn't possibly have ants in the numbers and densities she was seeing. It took the Australian scientist a couple of years to convince her that just because something was true for ants in the deserts of Arizona it need not be true in the antipodes. The American scientist had been victimized by what she learned first, and by the assumption that a theory good enough for ants in North America was surely good enough for those in Australia.

With little exertion I reach the top of the ridge and walk the length of a football field before being brought up short by the sight of five feral horses: a stallion, three mares, and a foal. I know that these are feral horses because I've seen this same band before; I know it because of how they run from me; I know it because no one around here lets his horses roam this far or this freely.

I think of Kevin and Angela, and I wonder if I could convince them why I should come up here with an automatic rifle and shoot this band of horses I'm now admiring.

I wonder if they could convince me that it's perfectly okay to blow away a tree full of galahs on a property down the road from the poultry farm because someone said they're part of the same flock that's been tearing up the Traeger Park Oval.

THE YEAR A CROCODILE ATE A BILBY

A little more than a year after going to the Centre, and some four months after a stint in northern Victoria and Melbourne, I returned to Alice Springs. The day I arrived I learned that Europeans and North Americans had recently condemned the Australian government for shooting feral horses in the Northern Territory. I would soon discover that no shooting by any government agency had taken place since the Love's Creek incident in April and May of 1986. Nor, I was assured, were any shootings planned for the foreseeable future. Indeed, because of a single horse lover in Sydney who had access to the press, some scientists with the Conservation Commission now planned to do a feasibility study to determine whether sterilization was a viable alternative to killing the wild horses. It was an idea that I'd encountered several years earlier in the American West. The Bureau of Land Management had found the idea to be very costly and ineffective. I was in agreement with their conclusions. But now, with news that foreigners, including my own countrymen, were censuring Australians for their presumed shortsightedness and lack of compassion for wild horses, my interest in the horse issue was rekindled.

Within weeks of my return to Alice Springs I had prepared a proposal to determine how to eliminate horses most effectively from a few choice areas within the Territory. With the written proposal in hand I approached a senior wildlife officer in the Conservation Commission. He had control over money for getting rid of feral and other troublesome animals in the southern half of the Territory. When cattlemen want 1080 to poison dingoes or a large quantity of bullets to shoot horses they call him, and he promptly fills their needs.

In the proposal that I handed to the wildlife officer I asked the Commission for expenses to assess the feasibility of a joint shootout of feral horses by pastoralists and the Conservation Commission in Kings Canyon and on several of the cattle stations abutting the MacDonnell Ranges. Most people familiar with central Australia agree that Kings Canyon is one of the more arresting and beautiful natural landscapes in the Territory. It has native flora and fauna worth saving, and some species are endangered. Kings Canyon also is home to feral horses. They linger and trample and pollute rock water holes during their periodic jaunts between Tempe Downs station to the south and adjoining Aboriginal lands to the north and west of the canyon.

In and around the MacDonnell Ranges there are somewhere between 25,000 and 30,000 feral horses. Too many cows and too many horses are ruining the rich alluvial slopes and lowlands around the ranges. Many people in the Conservation Commission, and many who simply love the Centre and know what's to be valued in nature, have been pushing for almost two decades to make the MacDonnell Ranges a national park. It requires no profound insight to see that the ranges won't be worth calling a park if the horses aren't soon eliminated.

I planned to visit Kings Canyon, do some footwork to get my own idea of horse damage and numbers, and then talk with the ranger in charge of the park. I'd been told that the ranger, of late, hadn't seen many horses in the canyon and therefore thought there weren't many to worry about. From other sources I gathered that he wasn't aware of the visible signs of horses in the more inaccessible northern reaches of the park.

I'd also heard that the ranger was overly sensitive to Aboriginal claims on the horses, even though Aborigines own no land and have no other rights in Kings Canyon. Even if some of the horses were indeed Aboriginal property, which is virtually impossible to prove, there was, to my way of thinking, no reason for not shooting them if they were in the park.

I wanted to talk face-to-face with four or five cattle station owners with properties that include portions of the MacDonnell Ranges. I thought that with a bit of luck I might be able to measure their willingness to get rid of horses. My motives for all this were pretty simple. I was starting to despair that any large-scale shooting of horses in the Territory would occur. Despite an offer by the Conservation Commission one year ago to supply shooters and bullets if pastoralists would pay the cost of hiring a helicopter, not a single cattleman in the Territory had taken up the offer. Now, despite bad press in Europe and North America, press that portrayed Territorians as a bunch of brainless nuts who loved nothing better than shooting horses from helicopters for pure pleasure, few Australians understood the need to rid the Territory of most of its feral horses before clamor from animal welfare groups around the world made it impossible to do more than sit in a lawn chair and register still further environmental damage by the horses.

The wildlife officer's sentiments about the need to get rid of feral horses were, so far as I could tell, virtually identical to mine. He scanned my brief proposal and said, "I see no problem funding this. When do you want to do this?"

"I'm free now," I said.

We discussed which pastoralists might prove resistant to getting rid of horses or putting out money to do so, and then I asked how much money would be available in this fiscal year for shooting horses.

"We just got the budget, so I can tell you." He gave me a figure. "Of that amount, more than half is for research and the like on crocodiles."

I swallowed hard, recalled that during the previous year there were a couple of whites who, through their own stupidity, had been eaten by crocodiles in the Territory's Top End. There may have been twice or three times as many Aborigines who shared that fate, but their deaths went unrecorded. Every death or disappearance of a white Australian or of a foreign tourist made all the nation's major newspapers. After every incident there were loud demands that the man-eating crocodiles be found and destroyed. The macabre stories were repeated again and again, to the delight of a public apparently convinced that it is far more likely to be taken by a fifteen-foot crocodile on a vacation to the Northern Territory than to get smashed to smithereens by a drunk driver on the madcap roads of Melbourne or Syndey.

"All that for crocodiles and then a miniscule amount for everything else related to conservation in the Territory," I blurted out. "Getting rid of feral pigs and feral buffalo and feral donkeys, a couple of hundred thousand horses that are working overtime to guarantee desertification of the Centre. . . . And then somewhere in that figure you've also got to manage to do research on everything else that's native in the Territory. Crocodiles aren't even endangered."

"That's right," he said.

Prior to 1971 there was an open season on saltwater crocodiles in Australia, and for a while there were fears that they might well disappear from several habitats. But as soon as crocodiles were protected, their numbers rebounded strongly. Within the first few years their population doubled. Since crocodiles eat their own kind, and most of those over three or four feet long had been killed by hunters, young ones could now grow to maturity without fear of being some larger brother's dinner. Once the protected crocodile population began to reestablish a natural size and structure, the population began to stabilize.

"The crocodile research is expensive," he said.

"Who does it? The Commission?"

"The money all goes to one person who's proven himself. He's published seventy-seven articles or something like that on them since 1973."

I guessed his name.

He confirmed it.

"Who makes these budget decisions?"

"People up the hierarchy. Politicians and a budget committee that has to report to people around the Chief Minister. Crocodiles get a lot of public attention."

I asked exactly how much money could be used for eliminating feral horses.

He gave me a figure for The Top End. "Horses aren't even on the list of priorities up there. First come feral pigs and feral buffalo. Every buffalo in the Territory has to be behind a fence by 1992 to protect the cattle industry."

"How about the Alice Springs District, the southern half of the Territory?"

"Probably sixty percent of the budget for this district can be used for horse control. But that won't go far. In the most famous shoot by the Commission ever, at Love's Creek last year—the only one the Commission's ever done in the Territory—we spent something like $20,000 to kill 2,000 horses. We took out several thousand donkeys and that cost us about $30,000 or $35,000. After one month, we'd gone through half our yearly budget."

I did a quick mental calculation and guessed that because of rough terrain it could cost as much as $25 or $30 a head to kill the horses in Kings Canyon and Tempe Downs. There might be enough money left over to kill perhaps a quarter of the horses in the MacDonnell Ranges. Then a year from now, given average rainfall, the feral horse population in the Territory would be greater than it had been before shooting the horses in the canyon and the ranges.

The conclusion to be derived from the new budget seemed obvious to both of us, so he turned to a smidgen of good news. A short memo I'd recently written for the Commission and cattlemen, discussing the need to get rid of the horses before it was no longer possible to do so and why it was necessary to move expeditiously, had moved a couple of pastoralists to shoot some horses. Within the past week they'd called and asked for bullets; they were supplied gratis. One cattleman was now shooting twenty to thirty horses a week, whenever he or his station hands saw them. By his own estimate, he still had between 1,600 and 2,000 to get rid of. He wanted to kill all of them. But he didn't want his name known; he'd had enough of outside interference from Sydney socialites.

Several of us at CSIRO are having afternoon tea. The topic of feral horses arises, and one of the technicians turns to Clare and asks her what she thinks of people like me who advocate that the Territory's feral horses be shot.

"I don't give a *damn* if they shoot them all!" she barks. "I keep mine behind fences, and if there are horses out there that are eating up the land then they should be shot."

Clare owns seven saddle horses, and when she's not behind her computer or doing other secretarial duties it's a pretty good bet that she's either caring for her horses, tending to those that belong to her boyfriend, or riding one of them somewhere on the outskirts of Alice Springs.

I snoop among those I've come to know in the Conservation Commission. I discover that the astronomical amount of money to be spent on crocodiles not only will go for research of no particular value, except to one individual, a former academic from New South Wales, but also will be spent for removing crocodiles from Darwin Bay and other areas where it's thought they might endanger humans. These presumed man-eaters are sent to crocodile farms near Darwin that were begun with the financial assistance of the Northern Territory government. There they breed. When they become superfluous or are no longer reproductively useful they're harvested for their skins and meat, which, I'd heard some months before, was beginning to show up in restaurants across northern Australia. Everybody's beguiling outback hero, Crocodile Dundee, had given rise to a whole new range of tourist paraphernalia in the Territory, including a "Dunto-a-Dee" burger, a roll filled with salad and a thick crocodile fillet.

There were now more than 10,000 crocodiles in breeding captivity in the Northern Territory. On one farm that has 2,000, the figure is expected to rise to 20,000.

I learn that the individual receiving money for crocodile research has a financial interest in at least one of the Territory's crocodile farms.

"See John Bertran in the Conservation Commission," I'm told when I ask if there's anyone who regularly works with cattlemen and has a dissenting opinion about the need to get rid of feral horses. I meet with John Bertran in his office. After a half-hour or so of wrangling that puts both of us on edge, he says, "You have to know this horse thing is an ethical issue. It's a case of are we imposing our position on a management system. If it's a private enterprise, it should be self-regulating. Many station owners don't feel they have a horse problem. If they did they'd do something about it."

One of the scientists in the Conservation Commission asks me if I want a good laugh. He hands me a letter that's been circulating among bosses in the Commission and in the Department of Primary Production for several days. The letter's from a group that calls itself the International Court of Justice for Animal Rights, with headquarters in Montreux, Switzerland. How large or influential the group is no one seems to know. I've never heard of the group.

The "court" has found the Australian government guilty of killing feral horses, and it demands an immediate end to such activities. The letter summons several prominent Australian government officials to make an appearance before the court and answer to its charges. Among those who allegedly have been served with summonses are the country's Prime Minister, Bob Hawke, the Northern Territory's Chief Minister, Steve Hatton, and several other national figures who deal with conservation and primary production matters.

In a document accompanying the letter it is claimed that horses are so close to man that to eat horseflesh is tantamount to engaging in cannibalism.

I've been reading *We of the Never Never*, an account of a woman's travails on a remote cattle station in the Territory in 1902. I come upon a line in which the female narrator says that it took three days to go sixty-five miles to the nearest pub in Katherine. The image makes me thirsty. I decide it's time to head over to The Other Place for a couple of beers and to surround myself with human voices.

I strike up a conversation with a ringer who looks and smells like he could use a bath and some clean clothes. He tells me he's worked on several stations north and west of Alice Springs. I ask him about one particular station I'd heard about, one that extends into the MacDonnell Ranges. I'd heard there were between 1,000 and 2,000 brumbies on the station, and that along with too many cattle the horses had been instrumental in causing massive overgrazing.

"I was there when the drought came on in '85. The bloke running the place is an accountant, not a pastoralist. Primary industry said he was supposed to have 4,500 head of cattle in that country. He had 7,500 when the drought came on. Middle of '85 we sold off 5,000 head. He had 800 head that'd died by that time. That's when he decided he wanted to blame the horses for floggin' the land into the shithouse."

"The cattle you sent to market: what kind of shape were they in?"

"We sent fifty-six down to South Australia. Twenty-six of them were dead by the time they got there, they was that bad. It was the worst record Tanami truckers ever had." He swings off his stool, adjusts the brim of his dark brown Akubra, brings a mug of rum coke to his mouth, and gulps it down. "He flogged that country so bad it'll take ten years to come back."

Steve Morton, senior research scientist with CSIRO, invites me to take a two-day trip to visit two German biologists who have been working with feral camels on Newhaven station several hours northwest of Alice Springs. We spend the better part of a day observing the camels, looking at the massive destruction they've wrought on trees in a paddock where they were enclosed for more than a year. That night Alex Coppock, who has owned the station for twenty-seven years, joins us for a campfire dinner. After dinner he decides to stay the night rather than return to his homestead. There's plenty of time to talk.

It's soon obvious that Alex takes considerable pride in knowing the native plants and animals on his land. He knows their scientific names, the time of year when birds come to breed. He knows several varieties of spinifex, has no qualms about arguing with Steve about how the plant behaves. He's laconic, a little distant, cantankerous. But he strikes me as reasonable. I like him.

We turn to feral horses, and he says, "What should I do with mine?"

"Try to sell them to an abattoir," I say. "If they're not interested or it's too expensive for you to muster them, then shoot them. Shoot all of them."

"I can shoot the studs if I can't sell them. But I can't shoot the foals and the pretty ones. I could take a pipe to the foals if I had to, I reckon. The pretty ones, that's another matter."

Twenty yards away from the campfire, his shorthorns are starving to death. He's losing several a week, more. I'm afraid to ask for numbers. There's scant grass on his station. Where we're camped there's not even enough grass to support a small population of granivorous birds.

We talk on, about our feet and legs being burned by the fire while our backs are as cold as ice, the nearby paddock where the trees look like they've been bombed. He asks me about ranching in the American West. I stress the problems that ranchers have had with feral horses. He hardly reacts.

The night grows long. One of the German scientists relates how a large king brown crawled into his swag and scared the life out of him.

I go to my swag, thinking not of sleeping with a king brown but of why I should care about feral horses when those who have control over the land don't.

I get a long distance call from Bill Synnot. I've never met him. I only know that he's the owner of Achilles abattoir in Tennant Creek, the only horse-kill plant in the Territory. About a year ago I'd read a couple of articles he'd written in which he detailed brumby carcass weights, the kinds and percentages of boneless meat he was getting from them, the number of carcasses he had to throw away because they came from gray horses and had melanosis.

He says he'd gotten a copy of my book. "I like it. You make it so the simple guy can read it. You make all those complex biological issues understandable. I was all scared of it. I thought it would be one of those academic treatises." Then he promptly adds that he's seen what I've written about the Territory's horses. He doesn't agree with me that it's a good idea to shoot them, eliminate them. "I see us as the middle road between you and animal liberationists."

I ask him to tell me something about his operation.

"Right now I'm dealing with over a hundred stations in the Territory. But they're not cooperating." He explains that he wants to buy 20,000 horses a year, his plant capacity. He'd be satisfied with 12,000. He's now averaging about 4,000.

He adds that more than once in the last couple of years it's appeared that he'd have to close for lack of business. To remedy the situation he's hired his own mustering crews to go onto stations with motorbikes and horses to yard brumbies. In other cases he's actively hustled business for horse runners new to the Territory. He's agreed to bring his trucks in and pick up horses where they're yarded and at no extra cost to the station owner. He's acted as an intermediary between horse runners and Aborigines who are uncertain where their money will come from if they allow mustering of horses on their stations.

"Is it true you've been trying to get station owners to breed up their brumbies, increase their size?" I ask.

"Yeah, that's right. Been wanting them to put out some good studs. They're not very interested."

Later he claims that he's being sued by two abattoirs, because they want his business. Then he says he's figured out his problem, why he's got legal problems and his business isn't growing as he reckons it should. "I'm not from here, mate. They see me as a carpetbagger, the mouth from the south." He cites an example. When the owner of Phillip Creek station, which abuts Tennant Creek and Synnot's abattoir, sees feral horses on his property he shoots them. He doesn't want anything to do with mustering or with Synnot's abattoir.

Before Bill Synnot hangs up he invites me to visit him in Tennant Creek, take a tour of his plant. Then, to make the 600-mile roundtrip more attractive, he adds that a restaurant in Tennant Creek is the only place in the Territory where you can enjoy some good tender horsemeat.

I obtain an interview with Ray Hanrahan, the Territory's Minister for Conservation. In the brief time I have with him I explain the need to eliminate feral horses in King's Canyon and in the MacDonnell Ranges. I express dismay with the priority given to crocodile research and the Conservation Commission's involvement in the exploitation of an animal not long off the endangered list. The minister ignores my provocation, chooses to focus on the issue of the MacDonnell Ranges as a national park. He says that I've put the cart before the horse. There is, he assures me, no need to worry about feral horses until the government purchases those portions of the ranges now in the hands of station owners. This, he says, could be ten to fifteen years away, if and when the government gets the money. I plead that this is an unreasonable amount of time to ask defenseless native flora and fauna to wait for rescue. "Surely the horses aren't about to suspend their destructive ways until then," I say, moving closer to his desk.

He doesn't respond. He looks at his watch and informs me that he's got a pressing appointment. Sensing defeat, time wasted, I stand to shake his hand. I leave reminding myself that this is Australia's crude capitalist frontier. I walk past his secretary and walls plastered with alluring posters aimed at tourists. I remember that Ray Hanrahan is not just the Minister for Conservation. He's also the Minister for Lands and Housing, the Minister for Tourism, and the Deputy Chief Minister of the Territory.

I talk with lower-level bureaucrats and workaday scientists in the Conservation Commission and the Commonwealth Scientific and Industrial Research Organization. I express my frustration, say that the feral horse issue isn't taken seriously in the Outback. One savvy individual in the Conservation Commission says that he finds nothing surprising in my complaint. Indeed, he's blunt in stating that the Commission is not, in fact, engaged in conservation. "The Commission's mission is resource exploitation. No one," he goes on, "is about to call his or her boss or the Minister for Conservation on this point. People want to keep their jobs. They want to upgrade their job and salary status at the first opportunity."

Those few scientists within the Conservation Commission or CSIRO who can't reconcile their own environmental ethic with bosses who care only incidentally about conservation retreat into less controversial research: identifying new plant species, examining the long-term effects of fire, searching for animals nearing extinction, doing resource inventories in national parks, working on elaborate computer programs only remotely related to the problem of overgrazing by cattle and feral animals.

I stare at my written proposal to work in Kings Canyon and decide that pursuing it further would be a Sisyphean effort. Feeling thoroughly depressed, I throw the proposal into a garbage can and head for the firm edges of the Todd River.

Before long I get hungry. I go to the bottle shop and buy two bottles of Jacob's Creek Shiraz Cabernet, 1981. I call Nancy and ask her to meet me at the Wild Water Restaurant. The Wild Water is the only restaurant in Alice with real character and unusual food. Few tourists go there. It's a hangout for vegetarians, Buddhists, punkers, peaceniks eager to close the U.S. spy base at Pine Gap.

When Nancy arrives I order some smoked salmon paté and brie parcels. I open a bottle and fill our glasses. We talk briefly about her research on zebra finches. I offer a toast to her successes, the fact that what she has found in Australia confirms that her astonishing laboratory results are not artifice.

Then I tell her a story about a jackaroo on a station far to the north of Alice and how he tried to steal from some of the other stockmen. Two of them caught him one day taking their cigarettes. They tied him down and then filled his pants with axle and bearing grease and mixed in a bucket of prickly burrs and spinifex. They tied belts around his groin to make certain that the burrs and spinifex did their job. Then, after they'd cut the rope binding his hands, they put a rope around his neck and made him stand on the sloping hood of a Toyota bull chaser. I get as far as telling her they had greased the bottoms of his R. M. Williams boots when she says, "That's enough. I don't want to know what happened to him, or if what you're telling me is true. Sometimes I can't tell if you're telling the truth or not."

"Truth is a complicated matter," I say. "It's always more complex than scientists would have it."

She frowns. "Tell me what you've been up to lately."

I empty the first bottle into our glasses, then open the second bottle of Cabernet and begin.

I tell her that I'm frustrated, that I see little hope that any major efforts will be made to save the Centre's native flora and fauna before there are more significant and irreversible losses. And then I try to explain, for Nancy, good scientist that she is, always wants explanations.

The pastoralists, I say, are hopelessly bent on maximizing short-run gains. They are quick to take umbrage when told that it is to their long-run advantage to get rid of horses and reduce cattle numbers and adopt other time-tested management practices. They behave not as custodians of public lands that are home to native flora and fauna that have preemptive rights over those of recent intruders but as outright owners of resources which have only purpose—to augment bank accounts. And because pastoralists and their ancestors have been in the Centre longer than other Europeans—forget Aborigines, for they count for little in most pastoralists' minds—they believe they alone know what is best.

If pastoralists were the only enemy in attempts to save the Centre, there might be hope for at least partial victories. Their self-serving disregard for other forms of life is constantly and relentlessly abetted by the Territorial government. The Territory's Chief Minister is convinced that all land abuse occurred in the last century and that present pastoral practices are not degrading the environment. Other ministers are either indifferent, ignorant, or, like the Chief Minister, so wrapped up in attempts to promote free enterprise and statehood and boost the Territory's marginal position within the national government that responsible environmental practices are left off almost all agendas. If a scheme or a Territorial venture makes money, or shows promise of doing so, then, *ipso facto*, it should be actively encouraged; it is, it is blithely and unconscionably thought, in the Territorial and national best interest.

Sadly, the Conservation Commission of the Northern Territory is a weak and easily ignored voice among those who wish to slow mind-boggling exploitation of the Outback. There is no lack of good scientific minds who understand the problems of environmental abuse and what needs to be done. The problem—or rather one problem—is that these workday middle-level bureaucrats have no power to bring about change; they do not determine Commission policy, nor do they have the ear of ministers. This problem is compounded by the fact that the great majority of down-at-dirt scientists feel they can afford to risk little. Almost to a person they hold to the tenet that to stand out or vigorously endorse any position that appears controversial or might slow rates of return on entrepreneurial investments will either affect their chances for promotion or result in dismissal from their jobs. Most are quick to remember a poignant example of an individual who has effectively been banished from the Territory for pushing a cause—no matter that it was scientifically and ecologically easily defended—that was unpopular or unpalatable to pastoralists and government ministers. Others, in particular those with CSIRO, those who can be counted among Australia's very best scientists, are culpable in another way. Rather than risk being censured for fighting the crassly exploitative norm with which they are thoroughly conversant, they flee into research and applied projects that are largely irrelevant to short- and medium-run ecological concerns. They shirk their public responsibilities in order to maintain their equable image and their comfortable lifestyle in what, in almost every respect, is a small-town society. They might not be blamed were it not for the fact that their mandate, implied if not written into their job descriptions, is to protect the public interest.

No doubt, I now tell Nancy, their reply to these kinds of harsh criticisms is that I am an outsider, one who has no family or personal future at stake in the Centre—an outspoken, impatient Yank, no less. I plead guilty, for they are, of course, right. Talk is cheap. And it is, isn't it, always so much easier to tell someone else to put himself at risk? But then isn't this the response that we all give when singled out for our shortcomings, for failings that we only admit to in private or not at all. Surely, though, nothing is gained by energy spent on lambasting self-righteous interlopers; it is time best spent saving the Centre's fast-disappearing natives.

There are yet other rationalizations they will use to counter my criticisms. We—meaning the scientists of the Centre—don't yet know that much about the environment. We are still in the inventory stage. We have to be careful not to give wrong advice, for pastoralists always remember those instances when we were in error; they are quick to remind us of past mistakes when we proposed something new and different. Furthermore, these scientists will say, the environment of the Centre often surprises us; some plants aren't—counter to expectations—killed with abusive grazing practices. Other plants rebound to a greater extent than was thought possible. Give us time! they say.

Say this not to me, I would respond, but to species approaching extinction!

Do we ever have *enough* information? How is anyone going to bring back life that can no longer reproduce itself? We cannot do so precisely because scientists and government honchos once argued that they didn't know enough, that their answers were incomplete. Because they were afraid to occasionally find themselves making erroneous predictions, giving advice that was not timeless.

"This is nothing but temporizing," I shout across the table at Nancy. "Intellectual machinations in the service of cowardice," I say, pounding the table, reminding Nancy, and myself, that I am easily excited. Not exactly the most diplomatic of messengers.

And what can be expected from the public? I now ask, ready to give Nancy an answer before she can respond. Little, I say. For no different than our public back home, the Australian public is almost totally ignorant of what this land once looked like, or how it might look were pastoralists and others to behave more responsibly. Only the tiniest fraction of the public has any idea of how the land is being raped and how native plants and animals and irreplaceable soil are being lost forever. The public surely doesn't care about soil, or understand that without it there is no life. And even if it did know about the dozens of small and seldom-seen desert mammals and plants on their way to extinction they probably would not give a hoot. The Centre's endangered animals are not large and furry and sexy; they are hard to find, and they are hardly photogenic.

As for Australia's conservationists, some of whom are very active and have done much elsewhere in the country that is commendable, the Centre is low on their list of priorities. And maybe this is as it should be. The Outback, after all, is not seen as among Australia's most attractive or fetching landscapes. Maybe—I don't know—it does not even legitimately rank very high on a list of environments worth saving, given all the problems elsewhere in Australia. But then shouldn't the Outback receive more attention from conservationists, if only because it encompasses some two-thirds of this gigantic land mass?

"You've painted a pretty hopeless picture," Nancy says. "Is there no way in which you can envision positive change?"

"Only if you allow me my cynicism," I say. "Allow me to advocate some things that a good scientist like you might take offense at."

"Go on," she says, after reminding me how much she has enjoyed her sabbatical year in Australia, most of it in the Centre.

I tell her that, though I continue to believe that encouraging Aborigines to return to their ancestral homes has undesirable consequences for future generations of Aborigines and might well create rural slums that are difficult to extricate or turn around, I sometimes entertain the thought that not only could I be wrong in imagining how Aborigines will cope with the twenty-first century but that I hope I will be. In moments in which I despair for the land and its true natives I hope that Aborigines indeed eventually find themselves owning all of the Territory. "At times, nothing quite sounds so good to me as hearing that another Aboriginal cattle station is failing," I say. With each failure a thousand or more square miles of the Centre becomes a potential refuge for endangered species. A chance—albeit small—for a hunk of land to be taken off the hopeless list.

I refill our glasses, then briefly tell Nancy what I told scientists at CSIRO when they solicited my views on what I had concluded now that my stay in the Centre was coming to an end.

I told them pretty much what I had just told Nancy, and then I added that they should not be so pure and high-minded about their science. There is one truth—a so-called replicable truth—that all scientists of repute worry about when publishing in scientific journals. But there is another "truth" that scientists—at least in their role as custodians of public resources—ought to be embracing when dealing with rapidly disappearing species and with humans whose mind-set is singularly exploitative. What's not needed, I told them, are more two-, and three-, and four-year studies on feral horses or rabbits or burning practices to demonstrate in good scientific form what is already known and obvious to the intelligent eye. All this good "academic science" is not needed before pastoralists can be advised how to properly manage the public commons. Accept the fact that you're going to be wrong some percentage of time. Accept the fact that your "facts" are not good enough for publication in scientific journals but that they're plenty good enough to advise those who are clearly not doing what is best for the common good. These "second-class facts" are more than good enough for those who cannot distinguish poor science from good fiction and who, in any event, haughtily rape the commons by invoking their own fictions. Endangered species cannot wait for scientific truths to be impeccable—which they never are.

I said that scientists ought to be brought to the Centre on term contracts, told at the outset that they have no personal future in the Centre and that their specific task is to tackle contentious issues and recalcitrant pastoralists and bureaucrats. If they know that they have no real stake in adhering to a social norm that largely precludes change, they might well do what others are clearly unwilling to do. If well paid, of course.

I said that an effort should be made to compile personality profiles of the most influential pastoralists, those who are "change leaders." The profiles might make it possible to identify the kinds of arguments pastoralists are willing to consider, and on just what points they are vulnerable to change. This would mean getting to know them on their own turf: in bars, at the racetrack, in the social clubs—exactly those places into which the Centre's scientists rarely venture. Is it not strange, I think I recall asking them, that the Conservation Commission and CSIRO do not employ people with a background in the social sciences or psychology?

I said that a couple of the Centre's most visible pastoralists and egregious land abusers should be singled out and energetically prosecuted by the government. This is something that has never been done in the Territory.

Nancy suddenly wonders out loud what I found in the U.S. when working on feral horses and how the situation there compares with what I've found in central Australia. "Is the Bureau of Land Management any more responsive to the needs of the environment?" she asks. "Are government agencies less compromised by the interests of cattlemen? Are federal employees rewarded for speaking their minds, being honest? For active intervention?"

The situation is, unfortunately, strikingly similar, I tell Nancy. The BLM is populated with competent scientists and range managers, and yet it has done a dreadful job of completing required environmental impact statements, taking measures to assure that they're not above reproach. For decades conservationists and others have charged that the BLM has been a handmaiden to ranchers. The way that the agency has handled many aspects of its wild horse program lends plenty of credence to the claim. Nor, I tell Nancy, do BLM bureaucrats find themselves any less compromised and eager to flee when faced with contentious issues. I relate the story of Milt Frei, who, all through the 1980s, was the BLM range manager in charge of Nevada's wild horse program. Nevada has long had more than half of the nation's feral horses and well more than its share of the West's rapacious ranchers, many of whom have been eager to run more cattle than permitted by law. Milt Frei has long had a reputation for being abrasive and outspoken. He has not been afraid to let me and others know that cattle and not just horses have been responsible for substantial soil erosion and loss of native species, increasing desertification. But it was not until Milt gave an interview to a reporter from the *Los Angeles Times* that he found himself censured by superiors. Because he spoke honestly of the role played by cattlemen in ravaging the Nevada desert he was suspended from his position as director of Nevada's wild horse program.

By now I feel spent. I empty the wine bottle into our glasses. Nancy gives me one of her charming smiles, as if to say she's had enough of all these depressing conclusions, not exactly what she had in mind hearing about on this her last night in a part of the world she has come to love as much as I have. So, in an attempt to lighten the mood, yet not quite able to unshackle myself from the conversation, I ask if she wants to hear a story about a thirty-foot Afafaru Sea crocodile, the largest one ever sighted in the Territory, and how it crawled over 1,200 miles of scorching waterless desert to feast on the last remaining bilby in the MacDonnell Ranges.

SELECT
BIBLIOGRAPHY

Afalo, Frederick G. *A Sketch of the Natural History of Australia, with Some Notes on Sport.* London: MacMillan and Co., 1986.

Alcock, John. *The Kookaburras' Song: Exploring Animal Behavior in Australia.* Tucson: The University of Arizona Press, 1988.

Alexander, G., and O. B. Williams, eds. *The Pastoral Industries of Australia.* Sydney: Sydney University Press, 1973.

Berndt, C. H., and R. M. Berndt. *The World of the First Australians.* 4th ed., rev. Adelaide: Rigby Publishers, 1985.

Brady, C. H., and Kingsley Palmer. *Alcohol in the Outback.* Canberra: Australian National University Monograph, 1984.

Breckwoldt, Roland. *Wildlife in the Home Paddock.* Sydney: Angus and Robertson, 1983.

Bryson, John. *Evil Angels.* Ringwood, Victoria: Penguin Books, 1986.

Buffalo in the Top End. *Ecos* 44:3–12.

Burley, Nancy. Sexual Selection for Aesthetic Traits in Species with Biparental Care. *American Naturalist* 127:415–45.

Chatterton, Lynne, and Brian Chatterton. The Politics of Pastoralism. *Habitat* (Australia) 10(6):12–14.

Chewings, C. *Back in the Stone Age: The Natives of Central Australia.* Sydney: Angus and Robertson, 1936.

Davidson, B. R. *The Northern Myth: A Study of the Physical and Economic Limits to Agricultural and Pastoral Development in Tropical Australia.* Melbourne: Melbourne University Press, 1966.

Davidson, Robyn. *Tracks.* New York: Pantheon Books, 1980.

Davies, Richard. Kings in Baked Clay Castles: The Kimberley Pastoral Industry. *Habitat* (Australia) 15(4):22–24.

Dodson, John. The Changing World of Australia's Arid Lands. *Habitat* (Australia) 12(1):34–35.

Domestic Animals Gone Bush. *Ecos* 13:10–18.

Donovan, P. F. *A Land of Possibilities: A History of South Australia's Northern Territory.* St. Lucia: University of Queensland Press, 1981.

Duncan, R. *The Pastoral Industry in the Northern Territory 1863–1910.* Melbourne: Melbourne University Press, 1971.

Evans, Howard, and Mary Alice Evans. *Australia: A Natural History.* Washington, D.C.: Smithsonian Institution Press, 1984.

Eyre, E. J. *Journals of Expeditions of Discovery into Central Australia and Overland from Adelaide to King George's Sound in the Year 1840–41.* London: Boone, 1845.

Fenner, F., and F. N. Ratcliffe. *Myxomatosis.* Cambridge: Cambridge University Press, 1965.

Finlayson, H. H. *The Red Centre.* Sydney: Angus and Robertson, 1935.

Frith, H. J. *Wildlife Conservation.* Sydney: Angus and Robertson, 1973.

Giles, Ernest. *Australia Twice Traversed . . . Being a Narrative Compiled from the Journals of Five Exploring Expeditions . . . from 1872 to 1876.* London: Sampson Low and Co., 1889.

Groves, R. H., ed. *Australian Vegetation.* Cambridge: Cambridge University Press, 1981.

Gunn, Aeneas. *We of the Never Never.* Richmond, Victoria: Hutchinson, 1983.

Heppell, M., and J. J. Wigley. *Black Out in Alice: A History of the Establishment and Development of Town Camps in Alice Springs.* Canberra: Australian National University, Development Studies Centre Monograph No. 26, 1981.

Hill, Ernestine. *The Territory.* Sydney: Angus and Robertson, 1951.

Horne, G., and G. Aiston. *Savage Life in Central Australia.* London: MacMillan and Co., 1924.

Idriess, Ian L. *The Cattle King: The Story of Sir Sidney Kidman.* 4th ed. Sydney: Angus and Robertson, 1936.

Ingersoll, Jean M. The Australian Rabbit. *American Scientist* 52:265–73.

Jeans, D. N., ed. *Australia: A Geography.* Sydney: Sydney University Press, 1977.

Kelly, J. H. *Beef in the Northern Territory.* Canberra: Australian National University Press, 1971.

Keneally, Thomas. *Outback.* London: Hodder and Stoughton, Coronet Edition, 1984.

Maddock, Kenneth. *The Australian Aborigines: A Portrait of Their Society.* 2nd ed. Ringwood, Victoria: Penguin Books, 1974.

———. *Your Land Is Our Land: Aboriginal Land Rights.* New York: Penguin Books, 1983.

Marshall, Jock, and Russell Drysdale. *Journey Among Men.* Suffolk: Hodder and Stoughton Ltd., 1962.

Masson, Elsie R. *An Untamed Territory: The Northern Territory of Australia.* London: MacMillan and Co., 1915.

McKenzie, Maisie. *No Town Like Alice.* Adelaide: Rigby, 1979.

McKnight, T. L. *The Camel in Australia.* Melbourne: Melbourne University Press, 1969.

———. *Friendly Vermin: A Survey of Feral Livestock in Australia.* Berkeley: University of California Press, University of California Publications in Geography, vol. 21, 1976.

Meggitt, M. J. *Desert People.* Melbourne: Angus and Robertson, 1962.

Naipaul, Shiva. *An Unfinished Journey.* London: Hamish Hamilton, 1986.

Parks, Don. *Northern Australia: The Arenas of Life and Ecosystems of Half a Continent.* Sydney: Academic Press, 1984.

Peterson, N., ed. *Aboriginal Land Rights: A Handbook.* Canberra: Australian Institute of Aboriginal Studies, 1981.

Pick, J. H. *Australia's Dying Heart.* Melbourne: Melbourne University Press, 1942.

Powell, Alan. *Far Country: A Short History of the Northern Territory.* Melbourne: Melbourne University Press, 1982.

Reader's Digest Complete Book of Australian Birds. Sydney: Reader's Digest Service Pty., 1985.

Report of the Board of Inquiry: *Feral Animals in the Northern Territory.* Alice Springs, Northern Territory: Department of Primary Production, 1979.

Reynolds, H. *The Other Side of the Frontier: Aboriginal Resistance to the European Invasion of Australia.* Ringwood, Victoria: Penguin, 1982.

Ride, W. D. L. *A Guide to the Native Mammals of Australia.* Melbourne: Oxford University Press, 1970.

Rolls, Eric C. *They All Ran Wild.* Sydney: Angus and Robertson, 1969.

Rowley, C. D. *The Remote Aborigines.* Harmondsworth: Penguin, 1972.

———. *A Matter of Justice.* Canberra: Australian National University, 1978.

Sergison, A. W. *The Northern Territory and Its Pastoral Capabili-*

ties. Melbourne: Sands and McDougall, 1978.

Shute, Nevil. *A Town Like Alice*. London: William Heinemann Ltd., 1950.

Sowden, W. J. *The Northern Territory As It Is*. Adelaide: W. K. Thomas and Co., 1882.

Spencer, Baldwin, ed. *Report on the Work of the Horn Scientific Expedition to Central Australia*. In four parts. London: Dulau and Co., 1896.

Stanbury, Peter, ed. *The Moving Frontier: Aspects of Aboriginal-European Interaction in Australia*. Sydney: Reed, 1977.

Stevens, F. *Aborigines in the Northern Territory Cattle Industry*. Canberra: Australian National University, 1974.

Strehlow, T. G. H. *Aranda Traditions*. 2nd ed. Melbourne: Melbourne University Press, 1968.

Symanski, Richard. *Wild Horses and Sacred Cows*. Flagstaff: Northland Press, 1985.

Terry, W. H. *Through a Land of Promise*. London: Herbert Jenkins Ltd., 1927.

Young, E. *Tribal Communities in Rural Areas*. Canberra: Australian National University, Development Studies Centre, 1981.

INDEX

Abattoirs. *See* Achilles abattoir;
  Synnot, Bill
Aboriginal. *See* Aborigines
Aboriginal Development
  Corporation: cattle stations,
  138–39; homeless survey, 22
Aborigines (*see also* Alice
  Springs; Anzac Hill; Honey
  ants; Land Rights Act; Sacred
  sites): and alcohol, 15, 91–96,
  104, 126–27; assimilation of,
  129–30; automobiles and
  trucks of, 26, 136–37; and
  birds, 70, 146–48; burning
  practices of, 78; cleanliness of,
  23; on cattle stations, 30, 102–
  03, 128–32, 136–44, 171;
  concept of land, 11; definition
  of, 18–20; and dingoes, 116–
  17; and flies, 73–74; and
  garbage, 14; health of, 21, 70,
  91–92, 95–96; and horses, 54,
  157; housing, 22, 140; and
  kangaroos, 70; miscegenation,
  99–100; number of, 10, 96; and
  rabbits, 113–14; and racism,
  26–27, 93, 95–100, 141; Pope's
  visit to, 126–28; sense of
  vastness, 70; social conditions,
95–96, 98–104, 171; taxis, 25–
  26; technology of, 10, 19–20;
  town camps, 26–27; welfare,
  139, 142–43; and zebra finches,
  70
Achilles abattoir, 56, 148, 164–
  65
Alcohol, restrictions on use of,
  15, 92–95
Alice Springs (*see also*
  Aborigines), 86, 97–101
Allambi station, rabbits at, 120
American Horse Protection
  Association, 61–62
Ammaroo station, sale of, 133–
  36
Amoonguna, conditions in, 101–
  02
Animal Liberation, and shooting
  of horses, 34, 57–58, 162, 165
Animal Protectionists: at Garden
  station, 48–49, and shooting
  horses, 61, 162, 165
Ants, 5, 153–54
Anzac Hill, as sacred site, 17–18
Aranda, 97, 101–02
Arnold, Sue, 34
Australian High Commission,
  shooting of horses by, 34

ABOUT THE AUTHOR

Richard Symanski holds a Ph.D. from Syracuse University. He is the author of *Order and Skepticism* (with J. Agnew); *The Immoral Landscape: Female Prostitution in Western Societies;* and *Wild Horses and Sacred Cows.*